FIFTIES KIDS

Allene Halliday

Village Books Publishing
Bellingham, WA

Copyright © 2012 Allene M Halliday.

All rights reserved. No part of this publication may be reproduced, distributed or transmitted in any form or by any means, including photocopying, recording, or other electronic or mechanical methods, without the prior written permission of the publisher, except in the case of brief quotations embodied in critical reviews and certain other noncommercial uses permitted by copyright law. For permission requests, write to the publisher, addressed "Attention: Permissions Coordinator," at the address below.

Allene Halliday
312 South Columbia Center boulevard #85
Kennewick, WA 99336

Fifties Kids / Allene Halliday . -- 1st ed.

Dedicated to my sister Pat

This is a sparkling account of Seattle's lively 1950's entertainment scene that chronicles two teenagers' efforts to succeed as dancers against the dazzling background of night clubs, burlesque, and vaudeville.

The Showbox features prominently in this book. It was recently named a heritage site in Seattle.

Introduction

So why did I choose to write this piece from my younger sister Pat's perspective? There are several reasons.

My references are the diaries and letters we wrote during this period. Because of her interest in journalism, Pat did most of the writing and her accounts are more detailed than mine. Were it not that she decided I should write this story, it would have been her book.

Pat's version is more dramatic. When we started our performing careers, I had finished high school. She was only fifteen. At that young age, she had to make the huge decision to leave school and home to embark upon this adventure. When I imagined myself in her place, I realized how difficult this decision must have been. That eye opener convinced me it had to be her story.

In the end, however, what it comes down to is this:

IT WAS A LOT OF FUN TO WRITE THE STORY THIS WAY!

Prologue

To imagine what it was like growing up in America in the early fifties, you need to realize there were still small communities dotted across the country that were just beginning to convert to electricity. The San Juan Islands north of Seattle were part of that rustic group in 1951, when my older sister and several other Anacortes High School girls were crowned Cable Crossing Queen and Princesses. With local officials and the newspaper's editor, they went out to our island's Sunset Beach overlooking Rosario Strait with a bottle of champagne to christen the cable that would provide electricity to the islands. A cheer went up from the delegation as they watched the last segment of the power's metal casing slide under the water.

Consequently, television could not be in every home at that time. In addition, of those people who did have electricity, not many could afford to own this expensive innovation.

Fortunately, there were still plenty of radio programs to keep families entertained at home (provided they had electricity). Shows such as *Suspense, Grand Ole Opry, Our Miss Brooks* and *Fibber McGee and Molly* to name just a few.

As well, Hollywood movies were enjoying great popularity: *Singin' in the Rain, A Streetcar Named Desire* and *The Greatest Show on Earth* were among the many films that filled theaters across the country. How could that upstart television possibly compete with those blockbusters on wide screens with stereophonic sound?

President Eisenhower, who is credited with promoting the expansion of super highways, was still on the campaign trail and would not take office until the following year. Therefore, traveling on two lane roads across the country, often behind slow moving trucks, was the norm. It took longer to get where you were going, but the advantages were you had plenty of opportunity to take in the scenery and read the witty Burma Shave signs. There were no monstrous shopping malls nor countless used car lots with gaudy banners flapping in the breeze to clutter up the landscape.

Home computers and the Internet were beyond anyone's wildest dreams; computers were huge contraptions that took up a whole floor in office buildings and needed specialized technicians to run them. We got our news via the radio and newspapers; we corresponded by snail mail but could send a telegram in a matter of hours, if necessary. Of course, by that time there were land line telephones with rotary dials in every home -- almost.

For convenience, public telephone booths were strategically located for those who needed to make calls from train stations, restaurants, drugstores, street corners, etc.

As teenagers, my sister and I lived on a small island named Fidalgo in Washington state. In June of 1952 Allene graduated from high school and I finished my sophomore year.

That summer we set out for New York City, where we planned to become stars on Broadway. The World Center of Musical Theater!

Nineteen Fifty Two may have been a slower, quieter time than today, but it wasn't a time of no ambition. We had plenty of ambition.

Well -- ALLENE had plenty of ambition!

Chapter 1

Now What?

In early September, our recent plans to make it to New York City and become singing and dancing stars on Broadway had been abandoned. Back in the safety of our home, we needed to come up with a new plan for breaking into show business. Maybe we should try going only as far as Chicago or Hollywood or…

In the meantime, school would be starting soon for me and I wanted to make the most of what little summer was left. Strawberry season was over, so there was no chance of working in the fields to earn money for school clothes. I decided to enjoy the good weather by doing the things I'd missed most while we were on the road.

First, I walked onto the Guemes ferry for the 15 minute ride across the channel to my favorite island. It was a mistake to bring Daisy our toy poodle, though. My plan had been to walk along South Beach for a couple of hours looking for agates, those semi-precious stones sparsely scattered along our local shores. I had a big mayonnaise jar half full of them in my bedroom. Unfortunately, the little dog's legs wore out in less than half an hour; I had to carry her back to the dock. To while away the time until the next ferry arrived, I skipped flat rocks across the water.

Next I decided to pick wild blackberries along Oakes Avenue on the way to Sunset Beach so mom could bake our favorite pie.

She made the best pies; they always won first prize in local baking contests. However, when my bucket was almost full, I slipped clambering up a small hillside and fell (very painfully!) into a bunch of thistles and stingy nettles. Worse, my berries spilled down the hill and all over the road. Result: no pie, but plenty of iodine and band-aids for me that night.

The final letdown came when I went into town to get one of those big, nutty butter horns covered with thick, creamy icing only Fortune's Bakery could make -- except they'd stopped making them that summer.

I consoled myself knowing I would be going to school in a few days and see all my pals. Allene didn't even have that bright outcome to the miserable summer. Her whole world had changed and so had she.

Normally, she'd spend her vacation going hiking or riding her bicycle or swimming at Cranberry Lake, but not this year. She couldn't forget the trip's misadventures and spent what was left of the summer just moping around the house. I couldn't really blame her.

Our high hopes had been fueled by the rosy scenario described by Cecil and Delorez, our dance instructors: we'd primarily barnstorm our way across America, picking up plenty of performing gigs as we drove into new towns and found work entertaining in their local clubs, make lots of money on our way to New York and be stars on BROADWAY in no time.

Bad plan! Barnstorming in the Fifties was not as lucrative as it had been in the Twenties, Thirties or even the Forties. Now agents booked acts weeks and months in advance. Cecil had only called one agent, Spokane's Dave Sobol, and that was the day before we set out on the trip. It was insane to start out without any jobs booked.

The earliest omen that this adventure was doomed hit us the first night of the trip in Spokane when Allene came down with a humiliatingly childish disease: three-day measles. This bad luck forced us to postpone our audition with the booking agent until she'd recuperated. Three days spent languishing in a hotel room sure dampened my enthusiasm, but my sister's optimism never flagged.

That setback was followed by our initial professional bookings: our dance instructors were booked into the nearby Stateline Gardens for the week, but we were hired to add pizazz to the floorshow in a Kennewick nightclub. The Glamorous Halliday Sisters. Right! We flopped big time with our frumpy homemade costumes and clumsy straight-out-of-dance-school routines.

Even worse, we'd left our stage makeup in Spokane in our rush to catch a ride to Kennewick with a traveling salesman friend of the agent. Except for lipstick and penciled eyebrows, we went on barefaced: no pancake makeup, no rouge, no mascara, not even eyeliner. This was hardly the captivating look of a Betty Grable type movie musical star the club owners and their audiences expected.

After watching our first show's less than stellar performance of the cancan, samba and clunky tap dance, the manager demanded we stay in the dressing room between shows. Clearly we were just kids; that alone could cause the club serious problems, as if the fact we were a terrible act wasn't problem enough for the guy.

On the bright side, we made the comedian look good and we stayed the whole week. Best of all -- we were paid!

Reunited with Cecil and Delorez in Spokane, once again we headed East in their Chrysler station wagon pulling a small trailer full of costumes, props and drums -- all kinds of drums including a monster that was six feet, at least, in diameter. Even though our instructors slept in the crowded trailer on top of the huge drum and my sister and I were in the station wagon, our cash had pretty much run out by the time we reached Flathead Lake in Montana. Nevertheless, low on funds as we were, Cecil insisted that we shop for handmade Native American articles, because we would find the "real McCoys" here. According to him, it was an opportunity we couldn't pass up. On the outskirts of town in a picturesque tepee that was combination workshop and store, Allene and I chose two pair of beautifully beaded deerskin moccasins, while Delorez came away with a magnificent feathered headdress, as well as beaded moccasins. It was all we could do to drag Cecil away from the various drums on display. He finally settled for a headdress and a fringed deerskin tunic.

For sure, now we had to give up on our plans to reach Manhattan, but, still hopeful we'd find work, we turned South.

When we drove into Cody, Wyoming, we were booked on the spot to perform in the rodeo. This was more like it! It may have been a rustic setting thousands of miles from the glittering lights of Broadway, but, what the heck, we were singing and dancing for a big audience that didn't care how young my sister and I were. Instead of sophisticated New Yorkers, we were playing to cowboys, cowgirls and Native Americans who loved us and we loved them right back.

Our big finale featured Delorez, Allene and I dancing in our brand-new authentic moccasins on top of Cecil's enormous drum while he, resplendent in the feathered headdress and deerskin tunic, beat on an assortment of tom toms. This number brought the crowd to its feet. Afterwards, Cecil and Delorez were adopted into the Native Americans' tribe.

As far as our barnstorming success stories went, Cody was the high point. We should have stopped while we were ahead. Continuing South through Yellowstone and Denver, while living primarily on canned beans and peanut butter sandwiches, we managed to find work again for a few days in a rundown club in Juarez, Mexico. Had we been able to sing in Spanish and play castanets, we might have been successful there. As it was, we couldn't, and we weren't.

Completely discouraged, we gave up the tour idea and headed back to the Northwest. We made it home with less than a dollar in change to spare. That was mid-August.

Chapter 2
Revising Our Plans

Allene was bored. Sitting on the living room couch, she flipped noisily through the hometown newspaper and suddenly exclaimed, "Look at this, Pat. Six pages of nothing! Nothing at all is happening here."

"There is so. *Tea for Two* is playing at the Islander. You know, Doris Day 's new movie," I countered as I changed the band aids over my deeper thistle scratches. "Oh, and McDougall's Creamery has real homemade raspberry ripple ice cream this week." That was almost as good as mom's blackberry pie.

"So what."

"But you love raspberry ripple ice cream."

"I have to watch my figure."

"Huh! Since when?" She was not acting at all normal.

"Since I decided my waist should be 22 inches not 25."

"Mom says that's just baby fat."

"Pat, I'm eighteen. You're the one with baby fat."

"Well, don't get mad. What's the matter with you?"

"I'm supposed to find a job here; I don't even want to be in this backwoods town. Can you imagine me as a secretary, or a store clerk or anything else in this place?" She sighed and continued, "You'll go back to school and take dancing lessons, and everything will be fine and dandy. For you!"

I'd never seen her so sad. She picked up the Seattle newspaper from the side table. "Look, here's the *Post Intelligencer's* entertainment section. Seattle's got nightclubs, theaters, burlesque and vaudeville shows, all advertised right here. There's plenty of entertainment."

"So-o-o."

"Look at this picture. The Manhattan Cocktail Revue. It's been performing at the Palomar Vaudeville Theater for sixteen weeks and is still going strong. It's breaking records."

The revue was a great looking act. Four beautiful showgirls dressed in glittering Oriental costumes were posed around a dark, handsome man playing violin. Captions read: "world famous revue", "a cocktail mixed to perfection, bubbling with fun and originality", "a treat for the eyes and ears", and "a tuneful, joyful experience not to be missed!"

"WOW!" I exclaimed. "Wouldn't I love to see it."

"That's what I mean. Seattle's the place to be."

I had to agree. Nothing like that came to Anacortes. Seeing that ad recharged my sister's ambition; her old energy and drive came back. She didn't say much, but I could tell the wheels were turning in her head again. She started moving again. Calisthenics. Ballet. Tap. Even walking around the house with a couple of books on her head.

Mom noticed the change, too. The three of us were finishing up the dinner dishes one night: mom washing, Allene drying and me putting them away.

"Why aren't you getting out and interviewing for any jobs? If you don't start soon, the best ones will be gone," observed mom as she scrubbed a plate. "It's all well and good to be concerned about your figure and to keep up your dancing, but you have to be practical too," she counseled as she handed my sister the plate.

"People here know you were a good student. Prospective employers want capable employees, but you have to let them know you're interested."

My sister took her time wiping a couple of saucers, then some knives and forks before answering, "I don't want to stay on this little island."

"I'm not talking about staying here. I haven't forgotten about your dream. I've always encouraged you kids to make a career for yourselves in show business, but, for now, you need to seriously look at the jobs that are available in your own hometown. It takes money to make dreams come true."

She turned away from the sink and dried her hands on a towel. Facing my sister, she said, "Do you still want to go to New York?"

"More than ever, Mom. New York, Chicago, Hollywood. It doesn't matter -- but they are all so far away. It will take lots of money to get beautiful costumes, theatrical photos, music -- all the things we'd need. I'd have to work for years in Anacortes to make enough to ..."

"Nonsense!"

I kept quiet except for the clatter I made putting away the dishes.

"Mom, I'm going to Seattle. Maybe I could sing with a band or be an usherette at the Palomar or something else that's involved with show business. I'd make more money than I would here and be getting good experience, too."

"I don't want you going to the city alone," mom advised. "Stay here and work for a year. You don't have to pay rent. You can save what you earn. Besides, as long as I'm working at Penney's, I can help you and Pat buy the things you need for your careers."

So, my sister began job selecting. She'd dawdled long enough. The choice of available positions was hers for the taking, but they wouldn't last forever: receptionist at the local newspaper, teller at People's Bank, secretary at city hall or counter of truckloads of dirt for Frank Russell's Excavating Company. Allene might have chosen one of those jobs, too. If it hadn't been for the postcard.

Chapter 3

A Bold New Plan

When I came outside a couple of days later, Allene was sitting on the front porch swing absorbed in reading the postcard. It had just arrived with the afternoon mail.

"Who's it from?" I asked eagerly.

"Cecil and Delorez."

"When do dance classes start?"

"They don't. Our former instructors are in Davenport, Iowa, working their Native American act for National School Assemblies and ..."

"How can they do that?"

"They're Native Americans now, remember?"

"But they're not really," I countered.

"Well, that doesn't matter. They're booked until next June. Can you believe it?"

Knowing Cecil, yes, I could. He was determined to get back into show business. As a young dancer in Hollywood in the 1930s, he'd done pretty well. However, I hadn't enjoyed being part of some of his latest routines like all the stomping around with Delorez on top of that oversized drum with Cecil banging on tom toms and chanting in his scratchy falsetto. I wanted to forget the beads, moccasins and all the rest. Had to wonder though whether he'd added the wild animals he wanted in the act.

"How do you like that? And here we sit."

"Here you sit. I'm going back to high school.

She didn't hear me. "How did they do it?" she asked quietly.

Unlike my sister, I had happily settled into the familiar daily routine at home and looked forward to high school with its challenges. I'd be taking Journalism and working on the staff of The Rhododendron, our school's yearbook. Ever since my newsgathering days for the school paper in Junior High, I had enjoyed playing the part of Brenda Starr, the glamorous red headed ace reporter in my favorite comic strip.

When the first day of school arrived, I hurried along the wooded trail to the campus and caught up with several buddies who were eager to hear about my trip to New York and the theaters on Broadway. I was ready with a well-rehearsed story. Audaciously, I recited how we didn't make it to the East Coast as planned, because agents kept us busy with nightclub engagements here in the West.

"We worked all the best places in Denver, El Paso, Spokane, Tucson, Albuquerque and some smaller towns," I lied to my pop-eyed friends. "Time simply ran out. Cecil and Delorez had to get back to teach dance classes and I had to go to school."

"But," protested one bright girl, "I saw a 'FOR RENT' sign in the window of their studio."

"Well," I stammered, realizing my blooper, "Uh, Cecil did mention something about a new location." What was one more lie? I was already halfway to hell.

My much-anticipated school day had scarcely begun before it dramatically ended. During French class, a scrawled message delivered by an office clerk stated there was an emergency at home; I must leave at once. Running and stumbling, with dreadful thoughts of a sudden trip to the hospital for mom and/or dad, or the house on fire (I'd surely see the smoke, wouldn't I?) or my cat's having been run over, I made it to our house in record time.

"What's happened?" I demanded, bursting through the kitchen door. Allene came out of our bedroom and announced, "We're going to Seattle."

I stood frozen to the spot staring speechlessly at her.

"Phil Downing said The Showbox needs two chorus girls. We audition tomorrow morning."

Coming back to life, I demanded, "Wait a minute. Who's Phil Downing?"

"He's the theatrical union man in Seattle. I called his office today to find out about joining; he's already trying to get us a job!"

"But -- tomorrow morning?"

"That's right! We can catch this afternoon's train in Mount Vernon and take a taxi to the Mayflower Hotel. I've made our reservations."

Reservations? My ever-practical mind kicked in.

"Allene, how are we paying for all this?"

"Mom's taking care of it, of course. She's excited about this chance for us to break into show business, but dad isn't. He wants me to go to college."

In no time, we were on our way with our neighbor Mrs. Watson driving us to the train station, talking excitedly all the way, "This is wonderful. To think I've known you since you were little girls skipping down the street on your way to school. I remember taking you to your first dancing lesson. It's too bad your mom has never learned to drive, but it gives me the opportunity to be like a grandmother to you."

She stopped long enough to take a breath, then went on excitedly, "It's wonderful. You're all grown up -- well almost -- and going to Seattle on the train by yourselves."

Mrs. Watson was a terrific neighbor and the closest we'd ever had to a grandmother. In fact, if I could really have had one, I'd have wanted her to be just like our neighbor: pleasantly plump and cheerful, with neatly permed salt and pepper hair and able to drive.

However, today I was only half listening to her friendly chatter; traveling fifty miles an hour on the highway through the fields of the Skagit Flats was making me feel sick. Besides, I was unhappy about leaving school.

Dropping us at the downtown station, Mrs. Watson said goodbye and good luck to Allene, who thanked her for the ride as I rushed to the Ladies Room.

On board, listening to the train wheels briskly click clacking along the tracks, I tried to forget about high school buddies, French class and Journalism. Allene babbled on and on about being back in show business and how we would be chorus girls and save money for music and costumes just like we'd always planned. This time it was "in the bag". I felt dizzy. Why did I let her talk me into this?

Chapter 4

Opportunity

The next morning, dressed in leotards under our matching navy checkered slacks outfits and carrying our ballet slippers, we walked several blocks from the downtown hotel to our job interview at a small theater on First Avenue across from the entrance to the Pike Street Farmers' Market. The huge neon encrusted marquee distinguishing this building from its neighbors read:

MIKE FOSTER

TWO SHOWS NIGHTLY

Norm Hoagy's Band

The Sundown Girls

The place looked deserted and was eerily quiet. Allene tried the door. It was unlocked.

"Are you sure this is the right place," I asked nervously. Today I was feeling more enthusiastic about this new adventure, but it wouldn't take much to send me back home in a hurry.

"I'm pretty sure," she replied. That less than confident answer wasn't what I wanted to hear.

"I hope you're right."

We stepped across the threshold into an unlit, deserted lobby. Slowly inching our way along the dark incline, we tried to ignore the oppressive smell of stale cigarette smoke that had settled into the carpet. At the top we looked down into a cavernous ballroom illuminated by one spotlight. A bit frightened as well as blinded by the sudden brightness, we stumbled awkwardly down the stairway toward the tall, willowy form of a woman standing at the edge of the biggest dance floor I'd ever seen.

"Ah! The Halliday Sisters!" she announced, her voice echoing across the room as she walked toward us. "I'm Patricia Dean. Welcome to the Showbox; I'll be auditioning you for The Sundown Girls."

Allene and I stood staring at the dark-haired beauty.

"I'm sorry I couldn't arrange for any musical accompaniment; our pianist doesn't do auditions or rehearsals. If he weren't such a great pianist, my husband would fire him. As it is, we humor the fellow."

She laughed and added, "I could hum the tunes." Elegant and soft-spoken, well-dressed, gracious and gorgeous, Patricia Dean was the most glamorous person we had ever seen up close. She could have given Ava Gardner a run for the money.

For one crazy moment, I wanted to ask her if she used egg facials. My sister told me that's the favorite beauty treatment of all the movie stars. I tried it. Messy!

Allene nervously cleared her throat and asked, "Did we keep you waiting?"

I remained in the background taking in this woman's carefully applied makeup and her stylishly becoming outfit: gold earrings, soft green silk blouse, full black felt skirt and black patent leather pumps. Head to toe, she was the picture of sophisticated elegance.

I began to feel dumpy and dowdy.

Seating herself at a ringside table, she said, "Let's see what you can do."

Stepping out of our loafers, we carefully set them out of the way under a chair, then took off our slacks and neatly folded them over the back of the chair. In a moment we were in the ballet slippers bounding nonstop through every dance routine we knew: cancan, high kick tiller, samba. Just about everything we knew -- except our part in Cecil and Delorez's drum dance. Focused on doing our best and delighted we had so much room to work in, we didn't notice how our exuberant efforts were being received by this critical audience of one.

Abruptly, she stated, "That's enough, thank you."

We stopped mid-routine. What would come next? Were we being dismissed?

"Take a breather; you're working too hard and trying to cover too much space." Gracefully uncrossing her long slender legs, she stood up. "Dancing needs to look carefree and easy."

I knew it! She didn't like us.

"In any case, you're both limber and dance well enough to handle any of my routines. I do like your enthusiasm. You're hired."

Whew!

There was more. "You've got pretty good little figures, but something needs to be done immediately about your hair. Mousy brown isn't good under lights."

In a happy haze, we accompanied our role model to her impressive Grosvenor House apartment overlooking downtown Seattle and the waterfront. In a few hours she magically transformed us into a pair of glistening, golden peroxide blondes -- just like Betty Grable and Doris Day!

During the process, she advised us on stage makeup, "Get Max Factor's pancake in suntan for your base. You'll need to have lip brushes to use Mehron's lip rouge, Carmine, which comes in a round can instead of a tube. It doubles as cheek rouge. Your regular mascara and eyebrow pencils are O. K. for now, but false eyelashes -- black -- are essential. They make your eyes look bigger. Be sure to buy a tube of liquid surgical adhesive, too."

"Surgical adhesive? What's that for?" I blurted out. Was chorus work dangerous?

"We use it to glue on the eyelashes; the adhesive that comes with the lashes doesn't do the job."

"Oh -- O. K." I suppose I am the family worry wart. Allene sat serenely taking in all the information while the bleach bubbled merrily through her hair.

Before we left, our mentor said, "You'll make your debut as chorines at the end of the week. It doesn't give you much time, but you can do it. Meet me at the Showbox tomorrow morning, 10:00 o'clock sharp, to begin learning the routines and be fitted for costumes."

We hurried over to Mr. Downing's office -- The American Guild of Variety Artists -- to tell him the good news.

"Congratulations! You kids will enjoy working with Patricia," he told us grinning from ear to ear. "She's a great gal!"

The short, trim, neatly dressed union man was wearing dark slacks, a matching tweed jacket and a bowtie. He must have been about 50 years old. But he still had all his hair. He reminded me of someone. I couldn't for the life of me think who it was.

Doing a double take, he added, "Hey! Who does your hair? You look like a couple of showgirls already."

"Patricia just did it," Allene replied, nonchalantly using our employer's first name as though she had permission to or something. "We start rehearsing tomorrow; she plans to put us in the show this weekend."

"That sure doesn't give you much time. Still, knowing your boss, she has to have a good reason to be in such a rush. You kids must be O. K."

I hoped so.

Good grief! Was I getting caught up in this showbiz thing, too?

"Now we need to find a place to live within walking distance of the club," my sister commented. "We don't have a car."

As if she knew how to drive a car, supposing that we did own one. When dad tried to teach Allene last year, she stepped on the gas instead of the brake and they landed in a ditch. The Buick had to be towed to a repair shop and dad was laid up for weeks with a broken ankle. There wasn't much chance she'd have more driving lessons any time soon.

"Most of the acts stay at the Cornelius Hotel over on Third and Blanchard when they come to town. They get a good deal there.

It's only a short walk to the Showbox or you can take the city bus that runs nearby. I'll check to see whether the place has a vacancy."

He picked up the telephone and began to dial. Casually, he inquired, "What's she paying you?"

Oops! We'd forgotten to ask.

Chapter 5

A Whole New World

We phoned home from Mr. Downing's office to let our folks in on what was happening before we went over to the Cornelius to check in. When we entered this small, attractive hotel, the haven for show people, we saw several men and a woman step out of the elevator. They were a well-dressed group. Laughing and talking to one another, they strolled toward us. One fellow spoke up, "Where are we going to eat?"

"I hear that café over on Fifth and Olive serves terrific breakfasts all day," answered the woman.

"That's for me."

Breakfast? It was almost 3:00 o 'clock! These people had to be performers.

While Allene filled out the check-in form, I asked the desk clerk, "Are those people who just left entertainers?"

"Oh, yes. That was Mimi Hines, she's a singer, with Phil Ford and Corbett Monica. They're both comedians. The other gentleman isn't a guest here. He's Joe Daniels, one of Seattle's biggest booking agents."

Our neighbors were a diverse group: singers, dancers, acrobats, comedians, jugglers, ventriloquists and more. They came into town to play several one-night performances called club dates for parties and special events at the Olympic Hotel, Norselander and places like that or to perform for a week or more in vaudeville shows at the Palomar Theater. Then they'd be off to work the rest of the northwest's nightclub circuit in cities like Anchorage, Honolulu, Portland and even Vancouver up in Canada.

Seattle was not a nightclub town, because the liquor laws (called the Blue Laws) in Washington state were so strict that only private clubs like the Elks could serve liquor. With only one vaudeville theater and not much else in the way of work, variety acts did not usually stay in town long.

The hotel management had a special name for this fascinating group, "the night people", because they came in during the early morning hours after performing. In an effort to keep the other guests from being disturbed, the whole third floor was reserved for this nocturnal clientele.

Our very first apartment had a small kitchen and bathroom plus a bed that swung out of the living room wall and unfolded its legs as it came down to the floor. Voila! Instant Bedroom.

We loved it!

That evening, mom and dad drove down from Anacortes to help us get settled. Besides bringing a couple of suitcases filled with our clothes, they'd packed up a supply of linens, pots and pans, dishes, glasses and cutlery so we wouldn't need to use the hotel's. This qualified us for a cheaper weekly rate.

Mom came through the door carrying bags of groceries. "I know you kids won't have a chance to shop, so we brought a few things to get you through the week."

She went into the kitchenette and, standing on a sturdy wooden chair to reach the upper shelves, began filling the cupboards with cereal, canned tuna fish, sugar, fresh fruit, bread and all sorts of good things.

"Mom, you've brought enough to feed every performer in the place!" exclaimed Allene.

As we unpacked the bags, mom remarked, "This is a pretty small apartment. Do you have enough room to rehearse?"

"We'll rehearse at the Showbox," I told her. "Wait till you see that dance floor. It's ter..."

Someone down the hall began vocalizing with scales and arpeggios.

"Who's that caterwauling?" Our gray haired, crusty dad wanted to know as he settled into the only easy chair out in the living room.

"Sounds like a tenor. He's probably part of the road show in town," Allene answered. "It's here all week."

"I hope we can see it," I said. "Oh, did you bring our radio?"

"With all that noise, you won't need a radio," dad grumbled as he adjusted his bifocals.

Next door someone was playing a rhythmic Spanish flamenco piece on the guitar.

"We're surrounded by so much talent," Allene commented happily as she came out of the kitchenette, where mom was preparing fricaseed chicken. "It's going to be fun having entertainers as neighbors."

As she entered carrying a stack of dishes, mom inquired, "Mac, did you notice the girl walking down the hall as we came in?"

"How could I miss her? It's not every day I see someone walking on their hands."

I hurried to the door, hoping to catch a glimpse of whoever was doing that difficult stunt. "Dawgone it! I missed her."

"You'll have another chance. She lives here, you know," Allene said.

She was sure getting cocky!

"Just think, you two are the first ones in our whole family to actually get into show business -- that includes all your grandparents, aunts and uncles, as well as your cousins," mom declared.

Before we could feel proud of ourselves, dad nailed us over his bifocals and asked, "What's happened to your hair? Has it faded?"

I'd hoped he wouldn't notice. It seemed to be a good time for me to find something to do in the kitchen.

"No," Allene laughed. "We had it bleached. Blondes are glamorous. Look at Betty Grable."

"Or Doris Day," I added as I left the room; she was one of the few movie stars he tolerated.

"I like it," mom said as she set the dishes on the tiny table next to the window. "It looks very natural. You two should be blondes."

"You would say that," dad complained.

"I'd have dyed my hair purple, if that's what it would have taken for me to get into show business," mom shot back.

A tap dancer across the hall started practicing a series of time steps.

"Isn't it wonderful!" Allene enthused.

"Humph!" grunted dad.

Chapter 6

How to Be a Showgirl

We were making $50 EACH per week. That sounded like a lot of money to me! At home, I'd only been making 35 cents an hour babysitting. Mr. Downing had spoken with Patricia after we'd left his office in order to confirm that we were at least being paid the union's minimum wage. The next morning, we began training to be showgirls. Our new boss had the contracts ready for us when we arrived for our first rehearsal.

We spent the next few days working intensely with Patricia and the other two dancers: Betty Ferris, a bouncy, petite redhead and Bonita, a tall, buxom brunette with an unpronounceable last name.

If it had been simply a case of learning the four dance routines, that would have been a snap. However, becoming a showgirl entailed a lot more.

First off, there was the pure torture of wearing stretchy mesh hose that cut waffle patterns into our feet after a couple of hours.

In addition, never having worn a pair of high heels before, I needed to master balancing on the four-inch platforms used in one of the dances. With each precarious step I took, there was the distinct possibility of my being sidelined by a broken ankle. Allene owned a pair of heels she'd bought for her senior prom. Since she had some experience walking and dancing in the ungainly things, she tried coaching me.

"It helps if you bend your knees. No, for Pete's sake, don't bend over; you look like you have lumbago. Relax and let your knees bend. Only your knees, Pat!"

If I wasn't balanced just right, my heel slipped to the side, slid out from under the single back sling strap, hit the floor and pulled down the rest of my foot, still attached to the shoe, because the front straps wouldn't let go. This, of course, twisted my ankle painfully, and over I'd go with a THUNK!

Nevertheless, hands down, the worst of all was getting used to wearing false eyelashes. If they weren't on just right, they poked us in the eyes. Then our eyes would start watering. This blurred our vision and caused our mascara to run down our cheeks. That ruined our makeup, which meant we had to clean up our faces and go through the entire makeup process again: pancake, cheek rouge and everything else -- INCLUDING the nightmarish application of those confounded wispy additions to our eyelids.

Unpleasant as it was to wear the eyelashes, that problem paled when compared to putting the belligerent little things on. There were many anxious moments as we practiced applying liquid adhesive to the razor thin edge of the lash. Too little and the things would not adhere, too much and the lashes glopped together in a sticky unmanageable hash. Once we became reasonably adept in achieving this first step, we moved on to maneuvering the exasperating things into position directly above our natural lashes. Halfway up the eyelid was where they usually settled. Often, slathered with messy adhesive, the imitation lash refused to adhere to the eyelid at all. It preferred to remain obstinately glued to a finger. Other times, just when it was being set into place, if the eye blinked, the flimsy enhancement ended up crosswise on the eyelid or dangling from an eyebrow. And whenever the surgical stickum dripped into our eyes -- OUCH! OUCH! OUCH! This made our eyes water, causing the mascara to run, which resulted in -- what else? -- having to start the entire makeup process all over again.

Another headache we needed to deal with was how to fit into the costumes we'd inherited from the former chorines, Verna and Fern. Sure, the seams could be taken in at the waist and hips, but bosoms were another matter. I was not well endowed in that department. Taking in the costumes to fit this section of my anatomy was not the answer.

Showgirls are NEVER flat chested. Whether naturally or artificially, they are ALWAYS well endowed. So, large rubber falsies were sewn into each of my costumes. This solved one problem but created another. Suddenly, I was top heavy. My bogus bosom felt like an oversized pillow strapped to my chest. When I didn't remember to give myself extra room, I'd bump into things -- like doorways and people. Embarrassing! As if that wasn't enough to deal with, whenever I bent down to adjust a shoe strap or straighten a show hose seam, I was in serious danger of toppling over.

Positioning ourselves during the routines was another important adjustment. I was used to dancing with one person. My sister. Now I had to line up with THREE dancers. When we formed a square and moved around the dance floor, we needed to maintain the same spacing between dancers. In a line, our kicks had to be the same height, our heads had to move from side to side simultaneously, our arms had to be in the same position.

Easy, carefree dancing is hard work!

Chapter 7

Opening Night

Opening day arrived too soon! Although the first show wasn't until 9:00, Allene and I arrived at the Showbox in the late afternoon. 5:00 o'clock. We didn't want to feel rushed. Besides running through the routines while the club was empty, there were so many other things to do: apply stage makeup, struggle with phony eyelashes, curl our shoulder length hair, put on the mesh hose (making sure the seams were straight), pull ourselves into the form fitting red fringed costumes and get strapped onto the platform heels. When we finally put on the red caps (making sure the two horns were lined up properly on each side of the head), it was almost 7:30. Good thing we'd given ourselves plenty of time.

Thanks to Patricia's efforts, the Showbox's dressing room was well organized. Just inside the entrance were two metal wardrobe racks filled with the evening's costumes. To avoid confusion, each of the dancers had their name tags sewn inside each piece of their outfits. Against the opposite wall was the long makeup table with four chairs in front of it. Behind it, a large, rectangular mirror framed with lights covered by metal grillwork (just like in the movie musicals!) ran the length of the table.

At about 8:00, while we were in the club making a last minute check of floor placement, in strolled tall, skinny Mike Foster, that week's emcee/comedian, with Norm Hoagy, the Showbox's blond, personable bandleader.

The popular Mike greeted us with, "If you kids don't know the routines yet, it's too late."

"We're just ..."

Smiling and winking at us, Norm interrupted, "Never mind him, kids. Mike just wants you to notice he's arrived."

"Hey!" protested Mike as the bandleader gave him a hearty shove toward the bandstand.

We retreated quickly to the dressing room where we gulped down dry cheese sandwiches and some lemonade, being very careful not to spill the lemonade. Ruining the costumes, the very first night would really finish us. There was even a sign over the wardrobe rack warning us:

NO EATING OR DRINKING IN THE DRESSING ROOM!

When the other two dancers arrived shortly before showtime, Norm's seven-piece combo had been playing for more than half an hour.

I was getting nervous.

As they changed into their costumes, Betty announced, "I'm gonna check out the crowd. Should be a full house tonight; the fleet's in!"

Tugging her strapless bodice into place, she looked at Bonita, who was powdering her nose, "Are ya' comin?".

The two of them went out the door. I listened to them clattering up the stairway making for the curtained off area near the bandstand.

"How do I look?" asked Allene, as she fussed with the pert red satin hat on her head and checked again in the mirror to be sure the horns were straight.

Seeing her face covered with orange pancake makeup along with the bright red lips and cheeks was startling. The black eyelashes that reached up to her eyebrows completed the picture. Unfortunately, instead of looking like a glamorous showgirl, she looked like a comical scarecrow! I couldn't tell her that.

Besides, I was pretty sure I didn't look any better. My lame reply was, "Okay, I guess."

Betty poked her head in the door. "Aren't ya ready yet? Get a move on. Show starts in five minutes."

"After you," Allene said, with a sweeping gesture toward the open dressing room door.

The band had begun playing the last song in that musical set. Holding up our long fringe skirts so we wouldn't trip, we clomped awkwardly up the stairs. Betty and Bonita stood behind the curtain calmly pulling on their long, fitted gloves. We fell into line behind them.

Bonita said, "Smile. I want to check your teeth. That canned stuff comes off the lips real easy but sticks to the teeth and everything else like glue."

"Are ya' scared?" asked Betty, grinning at us. Her green eyes twinkled mischievously. Patting her short raspberry colored hair (could it be natural?) that curled coquettishly about her pixie-like face, she counseled, "If ya go blank, just smile n' keep movin'.

Nobody out there will know the difference. Don't forget to watch the curtain when ..."

She was interrupted by a drum roll and cymbal crash. Next we heard Mike's deep, resonant voice over the sound system announcing, "Showtime!"

Our dark haired, serious looking emcee told a few "why-it-always-rains-in-Seattle" jokes, then shouted exuberantly, "Come on folks, let's welcome the lovely Sundown Girls in a devilishly delectable number. There was a bit of applause, followed by the opening bars of our music.

WE WERE ON.

Chapter 8

Uh-Oh!

One by one each of the smiling chorus girls pushed through the curtain into the bright lights of the dance floor -- Betty, Bonita, Allene and, finally, MY TURN.

On cue I started through the now swaying curtain and got knocked sideways by the heavy drapery. The hefty material caught in the horns and dragged my hat down onto my face just over my left eye. I reached up to push the hat back and watched, horrified, as one eyelash fluttered to the floor like a spider hit by bug spray.

The music played on.

Throwing off the curtain, I lurched forward into the smoky glare. The others whirled across the floor in and out of the spotlight. Allene nervously glanced at me over her shoulder. I was late. Frantic to catch up, I hurriedly kicked -- and stopped. My platform heel was caught in the fringe.

The musicians continued to play and the Sundown Girls, minus one, continued to dance.

Hopping on one foot, I tried to pull myself free of the tangle. I heard people beginning to laugh. I tugged frantically at the fringe, lost my balance and toppled over onto my padded chest. Thrashing about on the floor like a kitten helplessly entangled in a skein of yarn, I struggled to get my foot out of the snarl. The audience's hoots and shouts had become so loud, I couldn't hear the music.

Angrily, I rolled over and fiercely yanked at the fringe. My shoe broke loose, but its heel remained firmly attached to my costume.

Still, my foot was free!

I jumped up and, with one leg four inches shorter than the other, I limped through what was left of the routine with the snared heel repeatedly banging against my leg in time to the music.

At the end of that nightmarish experience, I stumbled off the floor amid the ongoing roars of laughter and clumsily clattered down the stairs.

In the dressing room, Betty looked at me sympathetically. Then her eyes widened, "Ya' only have one falsie and its smack dab in the middle of yer chest, honey!" Turning to Bonita, she wisecracked, "Some people'll do anythin' for a laugh. "

Tearing off my hat, between sobs I mumbled, "I want to go home."

Allene, too stunned to speak, sat down at the dressing table. The shocked expression on her face made me feel even worse than if she had gotten mad at me or something.

Patricia came in holding the missing falsie. "You left this at ringside, Pat. I convinced the sailor who snagged it that it wasn't meant to be a souvenir ashtray." She patted me gently on the shoulder and added, "Don't take it so hard."

Mr. Downing called from outside the door, "Okay if I come in?"

Betty quipped, "Sure! Just don't try collectin' any union dues."

As he walked in, he smiled her way, "You've cut me to the quick! I only wanted to say you girls were great."

Coming over to me as I searched for Kleenex in my makeup kit, he said, "Pat, you're a real trouper -- nothing kept you from finishing that number." He reached out to shake my hand, "Put 'er there, kid."

Recovering from my embarrassment, I changed for the first show's final number. This was a crowd-pleasing cowgirl routine. The costumes were short tan skirts with matching bra tops. There was lots of fringe trim, but all of it was short. No problem there. Instead of four-inch heels, we pranced around in low heeled cowboy boots. It was a breeze. The trickiest part was twirling the lassos. Real lassos! Our arms and legs were black and blue from practicing with the ropes all week. It was worth it. The crowd gave us a big hand when the four of us began twirling.

YAHOO! I was so happy, I wanted to toss my cowboy hat into the air.

By the second show, I couldn't wait to go on again. That opener was called The Oriental. We danced barefoot. Our pastel colored costumes consisted of high cylindrical hats with gossamer veils, velveteen bras, bare midriffs and billowing chiffon harem pants. This dance was an Arabian Nights fantasy. Rhythmically clanking finger cymbals, we glided gracefully across the floor to the strains of exotic sounding music. In one section the four of us simulated a Buddha. We lined up in a row behind Bonita, who was tall enough to hide the rest of us. The crowd laughed and clapped when we began waving our eight arms about. Great gimmick!

The closer was an energetic football number. A tribute to the University of Washington's Huskies. This was right up my alley!

We twirled batons as we marched on wearing typical cheerleader costumes of tight purple sweaters, short gold pleated skirts (our team's colors) and tennis shoes.

Once we were in, we set the batons on the bandstand and squared off for the game. From the side, Mike threw out the football. I leaped to catch it and passed it to Betty, who kicked it to Allene before going into a cartwheel. After my sister caught it, she rolled over into a somersault and handed it off to Bonita, who started running downfield -- excuse me! -- down the floor. Shoving Bonita aside (which got a laugh, because she towered over me), I grabbed the ball and executed a one handed walkover, which, let me tell you, was tough to do with that padded bosom. But I was bound and determined nothing would throw me this time! The first show's unrehearsed comedy when I fell onto the floor in a heap would not be repeated in this number. Happily, the acrobatics came off without a mishap.

As we took our bows to enthusiastic applause and cheering, Allene smiled delightedly for the first time that evening. Standing next to her, enjoying the unqualified appreciation of this audience, I began to understand why she was so gung-ho about show business.

Chapter 9

Carrying On

I didn't sleep well, because I was still so excited about our opening night. Besides, I knew I had to get up early to be first in line at the while-you-wait shoe repair shop.

The shoe man behind the counter nodded his head when I told him, "Please fasten that heel back on good. I'm rough on shoes."

I sat down to wait on a chair next to the shop window. After an hour or so of watching the traffic go by and browsing through all the old magazines on the table next to me, the repairman called out, "Kiddo, I nailed it first, then attached a steel plate. Believe me, your ankle will break before that 4-inch platform heel snaps again."

Wonderful! Or was it?

As I paid the bill, he asked, "What were you doing with these heels? Driving nails?"

"I was dancing, and I fell, that's all. Chorus girls do slip and fall once in a while."

"Chorus girl? You?" He looked at me hard. I wished I'd remembered to put on a little makeup before I came out. "Oh, I get it. You want to doll up for a Hallowe'en party. That chorus girl idea is good with the platforms. I'll bet you've got a little tinsel and plenty of glitter to brighten up the rest of your outfit."

"But ..." I protested.

"Hey, I used to sell that stuff: imported feathers, sequins and beads from Austria. Then the war broke out and ended my little import enterprise. You'd be surprised what people used to order."

"I've got to be going, thank -"

"Believe it or not, a waterfront restaurant sponsored some big affair one time where the guests had to come as their favorite seafood. Some of those folks really dreamed up some costume doozies, let me tell you! I sold one old gal big silver bangles from Turkey so she could be a salmon with sparkly scales."

"That's nice, but …"

"Then some guy thought he could look like a clam. He wanted a hoop covered with extra heavy canvas. We had a hell-of-a-time getting the goldurned contraption to open and close so he could breathe."

While he chuckled at his story, I inched toward the entrance.

"Have fun on Hallowe'en," the repairman said with a smile as I opened the door and hurried out of the shop. Before the door closed, he yelled, "Come back again!"

That evening, we were down at the Showbox extra early again to run through the devil routine a few times in costume. It was practice, practice, practice -- especially my entrance! Hitting that velveteen booby trap started my string of mishaps last night. Straight on or sideways, leading with the elbow or the shoulder, I burst through the troublemaker curtain without a hitch every time. As we were practicing the dance itself, we were interrupted.

"You kids want a spotlight?"

Startled, we stopped and stared into the darkened room. Who was it? Coming down the stairs to the dance floor was the bustling, all around work horse, Harmon. Stagehand, janitor, caretaker, and permanent fixture at the Showbox.

"Makes-a-hell-of-a-difference," he advised us.

"Wonderful!" shouted Allene. Today she was more like her optimistic self again. Throughout our rehearsal, she didn't seem at all worried about tonight's show and my performance. That gave my confidence a terrific boost.

After going back to take care of the lighting, the balding handyman in his old coveralls and baggy sweater cautioned us not to look directly into the spotlight. Then he sat at ringside watching us as we finished up the routine.

"If you're ready for a break, can I get you kids a coke or something?"

"Just water, thanks," Allene told him. Neither of us ever had cared much for soft drinks, which were the only drinks the Showbox could serve. Patricia had explained to us that in Washington, the Blue Laws did not allow liquor to be sold in public clubs. However, customers could bring in their own bottles of booze in brown paper bags and stow them under the table. When anyone wanted a drink, a waiter would bring over glasses, ice and bottles of whatever soft drinks were ordered. After he left the table, the sack with its contents would be brought out of its hiding place. However, the bottle had to stay in the bag while the drinks were poured and mixed. Then, the portable bar was shoved back under the table until the next round.

When Harmon came back with our glasses of water and a bottle of soda for himself, he pulled up a chair, turned it around and sat down on it backwards. With his crossed arms resting on the back of the chair, he leaned over to peer at us through his horned rim glasses.

"I've been around show people most of my life -- even worked as a magician myself for a few years. I can tell you, this is a wonderful way to make a living -- IF you can make a living at it. Nowadays it's getting harder and harder."

"Why's that?" Allene asked.

"Mainly because vaudeville is dead here in the States. Oh, I know we have the Palomar Theater, but it's one of the last. There used to be as many vaudeville houses as there are movie theaters now."

That was hard to believe. There had to be at least one movie theater in just about every little town across the country -- and lots more in the cities!

Harmon read our startled expressions accurately.

"It's true. Think about it -- thousands of vaudeville theaters. In fact, most of today's movie theaters used to be vaudeville houses. If they have real stages, you can bet they once booked live acts. You don't need a stage to show a movie!"

He was just getting warmed up. "Can you imagine how much work there was for acts in those days? Years ago, when I was a kid, I could see a show with eight or more different acts: magicians, acrobats, singers and dancers, jugglers, you name it. And the next week there would be a whole new roster of entertainers performing in my hometown theater. That's the way it was all over the country; thousands of theaters booking eight different acts every week. There's nothing to compare to that many jobs for performers these days." He took a sip of his soda, shook his head and sighed. "Have you kids ever seen a vaudeville show?"

"No. But we've seen movies about them with Judy Garland and Gene Kelly. What a wonderful...", my sister enthused.

"Movies can't begin to show you what the real thing was like. It was like nothing you'll ever see today -- except at the Palomar and a few other theaters where vaudeville is still performed."

"Gosh!" This conversation was making me have qualms again about our chances of being successful in show business.

"Some of the old-time vaudevillians have moved into nightclubs and are doing pretty well, but it's not the same as working in a theater. Anyone'll tells you that nothing these days compares to working in vaudeville. It was great!"

He must have been getting to Allene too; she stood up suddenly and turned to me, "Pat, we have to get started on our makeup."

"Time sure flies, don't it," Harmon remarked as he turned his chair back around and set it next to the table.

INTERMISSION

Let's take a break from the storyline to discuss vaudeville a bit more. Harmon does a good job giving the kids an idea of what it was like when vaudeville was popular in this country -- but there's more.

Although for close to a century it was a major form of entertainment in the U. S., now it has been pretty much forgotten. Many young people have never even heard of it. Its remarkable story should not remain buried in the past.

Vaudeville was a unique type of variety show. It began in Europe centuries ago as entertainment at festivals using local musicians, acrobats, jugglers and so forth. One version of its history claims that the name is derived from three French words, Vau de Ville, which loosely translate to "music of the town". When this entertainment form crossed the Atlantic to America, we pushed the three words together and it became -- Vaudeville.

Other shows of the variety genre are burlesque (which originated in vaudeville), circuses, revues and follies. What set vaudeville apart from the others was that each act in the show was independent; vaudeville was not a unit like the other variety shows which are made up of performers who rehearse, perform and travel together. Instead, the individual acts came from various locations around the country to a town to perform together in a program for a week or so; then each act would go off to other towns or cities to perform with a different set of entertainers. It was possible for performers to meet up on the road and work together again -- occasionally even forming a team, but this wasn't the norm.

Something all the acts had in common, however, were the vaudeville comedy bits. For some reason, certain comedy routines became standard fare. They wouldn't be performed in every show; just often enough that all the acts knew them. Variations did develop, but basically, they were the same routines. Interestingly, this is how Bob Hope and Bing Crosby first began working together. They were separate acts, who occasionally played the same theater. If time permitted, they'd do a couple of the old bits besides their own individual acts. This did not make them a team; that occurred when Hollywood paired them years later in the hilarious series of "Road" movies of the 1940s. Their rapport was exceptional, as easygoing as though they actually had been the lifelong buddies they portrayed. Furthermore, the comedic timing of these two vaudeville veterans was exquisite. Their background was so vital to the success of that series, they hired another former vaudevillian to create special material for each of them separate from the regular script. Often the apparent spur of the moment ad libs and asides came so fast and were so funny, poor Dorothy Lamour, their co-star, was left not knowing what to do next.

One popular vaudeville bit that burlesque borrowed and made its own was "The Old Lady". This routine was featured in the 1980s Broadway musical, *Sugar Babies*, that satirized a burlesque show.

Here's a sample version of that bit:

The emcee comes onstage and tells the audience that he and a couple of fellows in the band had been rehearsing in the old shed out back of the theater and they had a song they wanted to perform. This would be the premiere performance of the -- TA DA -- SHEDHOUSE THREE. The band members join him to form the trio, which is interrupted when a lovely, shapely lady wearing a sparkling leotard with a feather boa around her shoulders walks onstage twirling a tiny purse. She drops it in front of the fellows, one of whom steps forward to retrieve it for her. She looks inside the purse, then smiles at him and flirtatiously flutters her long eyelashes as she says, "Goodness me! All my life savings and you didn't touch a penny."

She starts offstage swinging her hips and twirling her purse saying, "Just for that you can meet 'round the corner in a half an hour, meet me 'round the corner in a half an hour."

Off he goes!

The emcee thfen announces, "You will now hear the first performance of the Shed House Two." Once again, they begin singing and -- guess what? -- they are interrupted by another lovely woman twirling her purse and, yes, here we go again! The other band member follows her off.

So, the emcee begins singing alone and HE is interrupted. However, this woman has on a well-worn old cloche pulled down so the tops of her ears are bent over and stick out under the hat, she wears huge horn rimmed glasses and fake buck teeth protrude from her mouth. Her dress is an ankle-length, shapeless, drab affair and her boa is molting all over the stage. To complete the outfit, she has on clunky, beat up boots and carries an oversized handbag, which she drops on the emcee's foot with a loud THUNK.

The patter between them goes something like this:

Emcee: What's that on your neck?

Old Woman: It's a mole.

Emcee: It's walking around.

Emcee: Can you do anything? Maybe sing a...

Old Woman: I cry when I sing.

Emcee: Oh, that's too bad. Why is that?

Old Woman: I can't sing.

Emcee: Oh, for heaven's sake! Can you dance?

Old Woman: Sure can

She goes into chorus after chorus of an eccentric dance routine kicking her legs madcap fashion out to the sides and exaggerating other klutzy Charleston steps. The emcee tries unsuccessfully to get her offstage before each new chorus begins.

The skit did eventually end, but it often brought down the house first.

By the early 1950s, when our story takes place, vaudeville was rarely seen in the U. S. Seattle was fortunate to have one of the last theaters still playing live shows. Harmon mentions eight acts in a typical performance. In the '50s the Palomar only booked four acts; the balance of the program was a feature movie. This kept the costs down for the theater manager and, consequently, the price of admission was fairly inexpensive.

It has been widely believed that the popularity of the movies killed vaudeville in the U. S. A. Not true! It was the depression of the 1930s that did the wonderful old entertainment in. Like so many other businessmen of that era, theater managers had to cut their expenses in order to survive; live acts were many times more expensive to book than a couple of movies. It was also easier for theater patrons to pay ten cents for a double feature than it was to pay a dollar for live vaudeville performances.

So, what became of all those well trained, extraordinary vaudevillians? Some went into the circus (lots of acrobats and animal acts began in vaudeville), some into the movies (besides the aforementioned Hope and Crosby there were Judy Garland, Donald O'Conner and the illustrious Fred Astaire), some like Jack Benny and Eddie Cantor chose radio and many, many more went on the nightclub circuit, which blossomed during World War II.

Still, as the old fellow said, "It wasn't the same."

From the author's personal collection.

1952 Christmas card. From the author's personal collection.

Cornelius Hotel
Seattle, Washington
December 12, 1952

Dear Sirs:

Enclosed are the pictures of our vaudeville type song and dance act. We sing in harmony and do rythmn tap, a Can Can and Latin American numbers with castanets.

We have been working for Len Mantell and Jerry Ross during our stay in Seattle.

We are opening at the Cave Supper Club in Vancouver on December 15th for a week but will be available to your office for nightclubs or casuals after that. Contact us if you are interested.

Sincerely yours,
The Halliday Sisters
Cornelius Hotel
Rm. 311
Seattle, Washington

Phone — Elliot 2888

Sample letter from agent

MIMI HINES   PHIL FORD

From the author's personal collection

HALLIDAY SISTERS

The Can Can costumes 1952.

The Sundown Girls with Norm Hoagy's band at the Showbox 1952.

Photo used with kind permission of the William Randolph Hearst Corporation

Patricia with the Sundown Girls, Bonita, Betty, Patricia, and Verna backstage at The Showbox 1952. Note the devil costumes. Reprinted with the kind permission of William Randolph Hearst corporation

Verna. (Pat replaced her) Reprinted by kind permission of William Randolph Hearst Corporation.

Official American Guild of Variety Artists notification

Chapter 11
What Next?

There were no further performance catastrophes; lights, platform heels, falsies, eyelashes and dances blended into a smooth routine. I was beginning to feel like a real showgirl. Now that we were more adept at putting on makeup, we looked more like showgirls, too.

Nonetheless, Allene and I continued to rehearse every day, working to perfect the carefree and easy look Patricia wanted from her dancers. Occasionally, Betty would join us.

I liked Betty. Having been with the show for a year, she was the veteran Sundown Girl. She also had known Patricia the longest; they both came from Phoenix and had gone to school together. "She and her sister Nancy started in show business when they were teenagers. That's when they joined a troupe called The Manhattan Cocktail Revue," Betty told us.

"Pat, that's the show I saw advertised in the Seattle paper," Allene remarked.

"I remember. They were performing at the Palomar."

Betty went on, "Yeah, that was quite a reunion for our boss. She introduced all of us to Jat and his wife, the stars of the show, when they came to an AGVA meeting."

"What's AGVA," I asked.

"That's our union, goofy. It takes too long to say the whole title -- American Guild of -- whatever it is," Betty explained, "So everyone just uses the four initials: A. G. V. A. -- simple."

Although I didn't much care for being called "goofy", this garrulous chorine hadn't said it in a really mean way. It was a kidding sort of way. So, I still liked her.

"How much longer will they be playing at the Palomar?" Allene asked.

"Heck, they're long gone. They got a terrific payin' job up in Anchorage; Alaska pays double what ya' can make here."

Hmmm. My mathematical mind started figuring what my salary would be up there.

"Of course, it costs twice as much or more to live in Alaska."

Forget that!

"It was a good thing they didn't get a chance to see our show."

"Why?" we both inquired.

"Patricia stole a couple of their routines."

Oh, boy! Our clever mentor just went down a couple of rungs on my esteem ladder.

Another time, after watching Betty practice kicks for a few minutes while we were doing warm-up exercises, I asked her, "How come you're not in the ballet?" Her kicks were so high, it looked like she was bumping her forehead with her knees.

"You'd be perfect," Allene stated.

My sister was right. Our redheaded friend was some dancer! She could make the most complicated steps look like "a breeze". Carefree and easy was the perfect description for Betty's dancing.

Continuing across the floor with her kicks, she answers, "Oh, I got tired of all the knee bends and sweaty leotards and practicin' for hours everyday. This is easier and leaves me more time for fun."

Seemed like a waste to me.

However, Betty could be a cutup in performance. She'd never get away with that in the super strict environment of classical ballet. Bonita told us how Betty's sense of humor could even get her into trouble at the Showbox. "Would you believe it? One night when we were doing the cowgirl routine, she came out sitting on the emcee's shoulders twirling the lasso over her head. The crowd was rolling on the floor, but Patricia went through the roof!"

As for Bonita, besides being tall, her assets included a great figure and the best smile in Seattle. To top off her attributes, being Latvian, she spoke with a beguiling foreign accent that devastated the guys.

On the other side of the slate, she had two left feet that couldn't tell a box step from a back waltz. Nevertheless, she had job security -- thanks to her popularity. This charmer spent the time between shows laughing it up surrounded by her rollicking group of regulars who spent plenty during the evening. Bonita never had to worry about her lack of dancing skills; with the crowds she brought in, any club manager would have happily let her simply pose onstage while the rest of the chorus took care of the terpsichorean chores.

Attributes like Bonita's are what separated the parading showgirls in the Ziegfeld Follies from the shorter chorines known as ponies. (All-around-work-horses would have been a more apt description for the diminutive, hard working dancers!) Being just barely over five feet tall, I gave up the idea of ever becoming a statuesque showgirl. It was impossible to find eight inch high heels!

We had seen little of Patricia during the last couple of weeks. Betty took over directing the chorus rehearsals. The few times we did see our employer, she seemed distant and unapproachable. At first I thought she might be disappointed with Allene and me. Betty assured me that wasn't the case, "You're both doing fine. She's just got a lot on her mind these days."

Knowing that we weren't the problem, I stopped worrying.

Still, we noticed lately when we came to work that Patricia's handsome husband, the club's manager, looked harried as he sat alone in his cluttered office by the entrance. The door was usually open while the lanky Texan, chain smoking cigarettes, worked on the books. He used to look up and greet us as we went by, but now he seemed too busy to notice. Afraid we'd disturb him, we no longer stopped in the doorway to say "hello".

One evening Bonita did not show up on time for work. The rest of us dressed quickly for the opening number and prepared to help the tardy dancer get changed. As we were putting the finishing touches on our makeup, Betty laughed and said, "I wonder what kind of excuse Bonita will use when that door bangs open and she comes bargin' in. She'd better have a good one."

Just then the dressing room door did bang open -- but it wasn't the Latvian. It was Patricia! "Bonita's quit," she announced. "Where's her costume? I have to change. FAST!"

Chapter 12

A Trip to The Rivoli (Burlesque, that is)

My uneasy feeling about our future in show business returned with Bonita's sudden departure; with her out of the show, our crowds dropped off dramatically. Even Allene began to worry. The combination of Harmon's talk about the scarcity of jobs since the heyday of vaudeville and the drop off of the Showbox's business were a double whammy to her career dreams.

Then, possibly to cheer us up, Betty suggested we go on an outing -- sort of. "How would ya' kids like to see Fern perform?"

"Why? I mean, sure, why not?" My sister replied.

"Is she the Fern I replaced?" I asked.

"Same gal. I've been wantin' to see her new act, but I didn't want to go alone. Who knows? We might even see Bonita there."

HUH!

When I saw the old rundown Rivoli Theater in a shabby part of town down by the waterfront, I regretted agreeing to come. As Betty bought our tickets at the cashier's box, I whispered to Allene, "No wonder she wanted company for this excursion."

My sister rolled her eyes and grimaced.

Inside, The old place was cold, dingy and smelled musty. Like stale beer. It should have been boarded up or torn down years ago.

I was sorrier than ever that I'd come. Seated mid-row center, surrounded by unshaven, drunken derelicts in Seattle's infamous burlesque house, we were out of place and distinctly uncomfortable. In front of the closed curtains, a baggy-pants comic rocked backwards and forwards in his squeaky shoes. With his hands stuffed into his pockets, he recited a monolog of ho-hum mother-in-law jokes. This red-faced little man's efforts at humor weren't well received. A pitifully few snickers, an occasional cough and a groan or two made it clear that the sooner he got off the stage, the better.

But he wasn't leaving before he'd had one last stab at getting the spotty, unfriendly audience warmed up. "I'm a little frazzled today. I had to take my wife to the doctor this morning; she'd gotten stuck in the toilet seat."

That brought a chuckle or two.

"So, after the doctor had examined her situation, I asked him, 'What do ya' think, Doc?'"

"Well, it's beautiful, but did ya' have to frame it?"

That got a few more laughs. They were quickly drowned out by boisterous shouts of ,"Bring on the girls!"

The unhappy comedian gave a brief introduction for the next act and hurried off the stage.

A tall, horse-faced female with long blonde hair wearing a full length sequin be-speckled chartreuse sheath and matching long fitted gloves came through the curtains. To the accompaniment of the theater's great organ, she sang a chorus of Rodgers and Hart's *Bewitched, Bothered, and Bewildered* surprisingly well in a husky, contralto voice. However, impatient jerks soon drowned her out with howls of "Take it off!".

Obediently, she began slinking across the stage to the muted tones of a blues song in an unsuccessful attempt to be seductive as she discarded bits and pieces of her skimpy attire. The stripper's bony figure looked better covered up. To applause that sounded like peanut shells snapping -- and probably was -- she left the stage.

I felt sorry for her.

"How much longer?" I croaked in Betty's ear.

"Fern should be next."

The lights dimmed as the curtains cranked noisily open revealing the golden statue of a shapely girl standing on a pedestal. Apparently nude, the motionless figure glittered in the spotlight. A loudspeaker crackled. Suddenly, the dismal auditorium was filled with the strains of Debussy's tranquil *Clair de Lune*; the gilded statue slowly came to life and gracefully descended from the pedestal to begin a slow, sensual acrobatic dance. Gracefully controlled front-overs melted into high arching backbends. Effortlessly executed kicks smoothly transitioned into sharply defined pirouettes. At the end, she returned to the pedestal and assumed the statue's pose again. The music stopped.

Silence.

The spell was broken too soon by a loud belch from somewhere down front.

The three of us clapped like mad, but not many of the others joined in. This bunch hadn't come to see an artistic performance.

Startled, the statue-come-to-life flashed a big smile our way during her bows.

The comedian/emcee stepped back out on the stage, applauding as he walked over to Fern. "Take another bow, gorgeous. That was bee-yoo-tiful!"

Before the next performer was introduced, Betty stood up and dusted herself off, "Let's get out of this flea house."

"Fern was wonderful," Allene exclaimed. "Can we go backstage to meet her?"

"Sure," she grinned and pulled her coat from the back of the seat. "Let's go. She has to scrub that gold paint off or she's dead. It's poison, ya' know; suffocates the skin. She's probably got one foot in the sink already.

Amid grouchy complaints of "Down in front" and "Siddown", we inched our way to the aisle and out of there.

Moments later, in the chill drizzle of that November afternoon, the Seattle waterfront smelled fresh and clean. I breathed deeply. It felt good to be outside again.

As we walked down the alley toward the stage door, my sister spoke up, "Why does Fern have to plaster herself in poisonous paint and work in this smelly dump?"

"Money, my dear, more money," Betty sighed. "Nudity pays well. She supports her bum of a boyfriend."

At the stage door, a blowzy looking woman sat behind a desk reading the Seattle Post Intelligencer. It was easy to slip past her and go in search of the dressing rooms.

Sure enough, Fern, wrapped in a towel with another twisted like a turban around her hair was just coming out of the performers' lavatory.

"Hey, good lookin,'" Betty yelled.

Fern almost dropped her towel. "Oh, so it was you giving me the big ovation out there. I might have known. Thanks! It's nice to have someone appreciate my efforts."

Betty gave her a big hug and introduced us.

"What are you doing here, Red?" The former Sundown Girl asked as she led us into the dressing room.

"Came to see yer act, of course."

"Yeah, right!"

"You were terrific," Allene chimed in.

"Fern, have ya' seen or heard from Bonita. She walked out on the show without givin' any notice. POOF! She was gone."

So that's why she dragged us down here! Maybe Patricia asked her to scout around for the Latvian.

"I haven't seen her since I left the "Box". Maybe she eloped with one of her fans," Fern said as she rubbed her short dark hair dry with the towel.

"Get serious. Ya' never were good with the jokes, ole girl. Better stick to the gold paint routine. Anyway, Patricia's been fillin' in for her all week, but business has dropped off bad," Betty shook her head and frowned.

"So, do you want a job here? I'll put in a good word for you." Turning to us, she added, "How about it, kids? Would you like to work in this palace of delights, too? A sister strip act would be quite a novelty."

She was kidding, wasn't she?

"Thanks a lot, but no thanks, pal! I thought Bonita might've followed ya' here. I guess she knows what she's doin' walkin' away like that. I'd like to wish her luck wherever she is. She's hopeless when it comes to dancin', ya' know."

"And good luck to you, too, Red. I'm sorry to hear about the "Box's" problems. Let me know if you change your mind and want me to put in that recommendation for you."

"Yer a good kid, Fern. Give yer beau a kick in the pants for me.

The gray afternoon magnified the decay and neglect in this old section of Seattle. We hurried past grimy concrete buildings, soot blackened broken signs and cracked shop windows. The litter of newspapers, cigarette butts and dead leaves lay in sodden piles along the gutters of the desolate street. Everything in sight conspired to intensify the depression we felt.

"Well, kids, my hunch was dead wrong," complained Betty. "No use worryin' about the crazy Latvian. She's smart enough to have stayed clear of that joint."

I was confused. "Why would Bonita leave without saying anything to anybody?"

The normally talkative redhead silently shrugged her shoulders. Jamming her hands into her coat pockets, she forged ahead of us, deep in thought. We trudged behind her, bewildered and dejected.

Stopping in front of the Showbox, she abruptly turned to face us and exploded, "Time to open yer baby blues. How do ya' think ya' got these jobs? Because two dancers quit, that's how. How often do yer think a four girl line loses two chorines at once?"

"Uh, I never ...," Allene answered.

"Ya' wanna know what I think?" Without giving us a chance to answer, she told us, "The Showbox is going under. We're already waist deep. Use yer noggins. It's practically the holiday season; the BIG season fer shows and we can't bring in a decent crowd." She lowered her voice, "That's real scary. Maybe we should be jumpin' ship, too."

Shocked, I spoke up, "We can't do that." We'd only been working a few weeks. We hadn't had enough time to save up for costumes and music and everything else we needed to go on our own. If we really scrimped, we had maybe enough to live for a few more weeks in the city. That was it.

"I've got to get somethin' for dinner," Betty said abruptly turning to cross the street to the Farmer's Market.

Unhappily, we stood for a minute watching her. I considered running over to warn her about the guy at the fruit stand who sneaks the old produce from under the counter with a sleight of hand that any magician would envy. Supposedly putting the fruit you hand him into a paper sack and onto the scale, he makes the switch and -- oh, well.

Allene, choking back her tears, tugged open the door into the Showbox and we went inside. From the top of the lobby, we looked down into the ballroom. It wasn't a warm, friendly place anymore. Now it looked as dark and forbidding as an abandoned coal mine.

Chapter 13

New Friends

"Hey! Look, it's the Dolly Sisters."

This startling greeting came from down near the dance floor. It took a moment before our eyes adjusted to the dim lighting and we could make out the figures of a man and woman seated with their feet propped up on a ringside table.

"Saw your show last night. You two looked good -- nice job," he commented. He stood up to pull out a couple of chairs. I noted that his physique was small, muscular and agile; he had to be an acrobat or a dancer. Maybe both.

"Come on down here, angels. Have a seat. I'm Lou and the sleepyhead is Camille. We're taking a break." His impish face welcomed us with a big grin. After the afternoon we'd had, it was wonderful to see!

At closer range I recognized them. If I was keeping my acts straight, they'd checked into the Cornelius a few days ago.

His brunette companion waved and yawned.

"Excuse her, kids. She's beat. We've been rehearsing for our booking at the Palomar; can't rehearse there, because they have continuous shows. Movies and acts all day long. Heard about this great room from a guy staying at our hotel," he explained.

"This is a monster of a room," Camille said looking sleepily around.

"What a Class A dance floor. No loose boards. Wow! We just came from working two weeks at a toilet in Fairbanks. Geez, you should have seen that floor! Like a postage stamp. A used postage stamps. Get it?"

We looked at him blankly.

"Wavy boards, all the way across; like wavy lines, see!"

Sort of, I guess. Never having heard anyone talk like that before, we were kind of in shock.

He burst into a booming laugh and slapped his knee while his companion glanced our way, shook her head and said, "You'll get used to him. I did."

"What a crock. Had to change the finish to our act. I do these barrel turns, see. Had to take those out. I'd have landed in somebody's highball."

And I thought Betty was a talker!

"That's the reason we wanted to run through the routine," Camille added. "Lou needs to brush up on those barrel turns before they go back into our act."

"Hey, I'm not …," he started to protest, but stopped to look closely at me. "Say, you're kind of young to be a chorus girl, aren't you?"

"I -- uh …"

"Oh, no," Allene broke in hurriedly seeing that Lou's rapid fire chatter had left me in a daze. "She's 21, I'm a year older. We look a lot younger."

"Sure! And I'm Rip Van Winkle," he answered chuckling.

"Never mind. Your secret's safe," Camille assured us.

Changing the subject, Lou inquired, "Are you kids planning to rehearse or something?"

"We won't be long," I said.

"Aw, take your time. We're probably through for today anyhow," he said looking across at his weary partner. "Mind if we watch?"

Why not? I was getting used to having people around during our workouts. Besides, it was pretty dark without the spotlight.

In ballet slippers, we ran through the Showbox routines and then some dance school specialties. The workout felt good and got us past the hopeless feeling we'd walked in with. Worn out, I sank to the floor, while Allene, hands on her hips, walked in a circle to catch her breath.

"You angels ought to do an act of your own," said Lou, jumping up from his chair and walking over to us. "Break out of the chorus line crud."

The guy must be a mind reader!

Camille stood up slowly, nodding her head. "Lou and I did," she sighed.

I noticed she was all legs and tall like Patricia, but not so glamorous looking. Maybe it was the giant horn-rimmed glasses. They'd slipped down her nose and looked like they were about to fall off. Over the rims, she momentarily peered at us with her huge dark eyes, then stifled another yawn with her hand, "Sorry."

"Yeh, geez! We did a bunch of boring musicals at Warner Bros. That's how we met; herded together for the chorus line cattle call.

Crappy way to make a living. We bolted after we finished *Tea for Two,* the latest Doris Day movie.

"Are you in that movie?" Allene inquired.

I did try to get her to see it. Wish I'd gone alone.

"Yeah. I even step out of the chorus line in one of the opening scenes. I'm the guy in the funny looking bathing suit jumping off the high dive into the pool."

I knew he was an athlete!

"Do you know any movie stars?" I asked just like a silly teenager.

"Plenty. They're just folks like you and me -- except they have millions and millions of dollars."

I liked this brash talking fellow. His good humor was just what we needed. He had us smiling and laughing at his chatter and funny remarks. For a while we forgot our troubles.

"Hey, let me give you angels some advice. You're good little dancers, but you're not working smart. You need to dance in unison. Cut out the mirror image stuff. It's hard to keep our sights on both of you when you head off in opposite directions. Are you afraid you'll run into each other? Keep your heads, arms, legs, everything, all the same. Dig? Synchronize."

His bespectacled partner spoke up, "Lou's dad and uncle were a dance team in vaudeville years ago. He thinks that makes him the expert on sister acts." She gave him a playful shove and, like a rag doll, he crumpled to the floor and rolled onto his back.

Comfortably lying there with his ankles crossed and the back of his head resting on his hands, he solemnly pronounced, "Hey, never mind her. Try doing your routines the way I said and see if I'm right. Deal!" Quick as a wink, he executed a nip up and was on his feet saying, "We have to be going. Keep in touch; we're staying at the Cornelius over on..."

"I saw you check in. We're on the third floor too," I said enthusiastically.

"Then we're neighbors; that's good. I'll get you some complimentary tickets for our show. You'll see more than the Mosconis. That's us, by the way. I hear tell that Lady Godiva, complete with a white horse yet, will be on the bill. Should be a sight worth seeing."

Camille gave him another shove, harder this time, and started up the stairs.

Stubbornly, he continued, "I don't care who gets top billing, but I sure as hell hope we get onstage before that horse."

"Come on, Lou!"

"Tomorrow's the opening. See ya'." He followed her to the top of the stairs. Before going down the lobby, he turned to lean over the railing, "Don't forget! By the way, the movie is *Winchester '73* starring Jimmy Stewart. That'll be...

Suddenly, a hand grabbed him by the collar and he was gone.

Chapter 14

A Vaudeville Show

As Betty had predicted, the Showbox closed within the week. Our steady jobs were gone before Allene and I had saved enough for new costumes, music and photos. This time, though, we were determined to strike out on our own, ready or not, rather than return home a second time as failures.

The bright spot of the week was that our new friends were as good as their word about the tickets for their Palomar show. Other than catching the Saturday matinee of *Oklahoma,* we had not gone to any stage shows in town, unless you want to count the trip to the Rivoli -- which we did not! Seeing our first ever vaudeville show was a wild, wonderful experience, in part because we were watching people we actually knew performing live onstage.

The band in the pit gave the opening fanfare and out came Arthur Ward, veteran juggler, in a formal tux. His young, leotard clad feminine assistant threw out hoops, handed him dishes, rubber balls and other paraphernalia, all the while smiling a charming dimpled grin for the audience. If anyone tore their eyes away from that cutie, they saw that the gray haired old guy was good. Darn good.

Next came a petite blonde singer poured into a glistening rhinestone gown. Mimi Hines. What a voice! It ricocheted off the walls as she belted out her opening number. That was followed by a slow, sexy rendition of Hoagy Carmichael's *Nearness of You* before her partner, chunky, cherubic Phil Ford, decked out in a checkered suit, joined her onstage.

They ran through several comedy skits. What we hadn't noticed when the blonde was singing were her prominent front teeth. During the duo's comical patter, she made the most of them, giving a super impression of a chipmunk. Further enhancing the comedic effect, she talked quickly in a high chirpy voice that sounded a lot like that rascal Alvin on the Chipmunks recordings. My sides ached from laughing!

When she exited, the comedian gave a clever impression of Winston Churchill, including his signature wartime "V" for victory sign made with two fingers of one hand. However, the vaudevillian's punch line was, "The cavity where once the body lay," referring to the statesman's famous cigar smoking habit. His part in the show ended with a sensational clarinet solo.

Then it was our friends' turn. Could they hold their own following those two terrific opening acts?

You better believe they could!

Lou came bouncing onstage to Cole Porter's *Another Opening, Another Show* looking sharp in a black tux and bowtie. We watched his athletic stunts wide-eyed. Jump splits. Barrel turns. No handed front-overs. Finally, he ran up the side of the proscenium and sprang into an astonishing backward flip. Landing lightly back on the floor, he took his bow down on one knee with his arms wide open -- like Al Jolson did.

Following the thunderous round of applause, he stood up, straightened his tie and announced, "Now that I have your attention, allow me to introduce you to the irresistible Miss Camille Williams."

Dressed in a sleek satin leotard that accentuated her incredibly long, shapely legs, the ex-chorine danced to the strains of Gershwin's *Embraceable You.* Without her horned rim glasses, she was drop-dead-gorgeous. Her effortless high kicks rivaled Betty's and then some, while her dizzying spins were out of this world.

How did Hollywood ever let her get away?

Wearing a straw hat, tight wide-striped tee shirt and dark slacks, Lou ran back on to applaud the end of her routine as she made her exit. When the audience's clapping died down, he spoke briefly about the thrill it was for him to be in this theater where his father and uncle -- the famous Mosconi Brothers -- had performed years before.

More applause.

Then Camille, wearing a short, jaunty, full skirted taffeta outfit, joined him for a fast, over the top tap routine. *S*ensational!

As for Lady Godiva -- I loved the horse!

Chapter 15
The Club Date Scene

"You kids have to get show photos to pass out to agents or you'll never get any work. I'll call some people and see what kind of a deal I can get for you," Mr. Downing told us after he'd learned of the Showbox's demise.

Think about it. We'd only met him a couple of months ago, he was the union man and he'd already collected his dues from us. Yet, here he was buoying us up like a life jacket in that sea of despair we'd tumbled into.

You had to love the guy!

Fortunately, it was a time of celebrations all over Seattle thanks to the upcoming holidays. Private clubs like the Eagles and Elks could serve liquor in Washington state. That fact alone may have accounted for the local popularity of those fraternal organizations.

If we could get enough club dates, we'd be able to stay at the Cornelius and afford to get show photos, too.

That was one big "IF".

Patricia wanted to keep the Sundown Girls working until the "Box" could pay off its creditors and reopen. "I need to work full time to get club dates for the line. I've talked Bonita into coming back for a few weeks to help out in the dances. Thank God she's still in town!"

The Latvian had signed on with local magician, Chris diJulio, to be his onstage assistant. Since the new team's first nightclub booking for two weeks was in Reno after New Year's, she agreed to help us out. With one stipulation. "Chris has to be part of the package."

At our first pickup rehearsal Betty's question for the brunette was, "So, what's it like to be sawed in half, sweetie?"

Our last night at the Showbox, Patricia said, "Let's make this our best show ever!"

Why not?!

However, right in the middle of our opening number, someone in the audience stood right up and yelled, "Pat! Allene! What are you doing here?"

It's Sharon Smith from Anacortes. She graduated with my sister. This was my worst nightmare! Someone from our hometown was actually in the audience -- and recognized us! Never mind that we had blonde hair and lots of show makeup on. We didn't fool Sharon. She knew EXACTLY who we were. WORSE, she knew how old we were!

Once I stopped to think about it, I realized that if this had to happen, the timing couldn't have been better. It was too late for us to be fired because we were under age; we were already on our way out the door.

Dumfounded as we were, there was nothing for it but to go out into the club during intermission and visit with our fellow Anacortesan. Result? No Drama. No Trauma. Even Betty didn't needle us about the incident.

I'm such a worry wart!

There'd been an earlier run-in with one of Allene's classmates at the Farmer's Market. That time it was Joyce Estabrook. She and my sister had worked as usherettes at the Empire movie theater during their junior and senior years. Allene bluffed her way out of that embarrassing meeting by telling her we were studying in Seattle. (Which was only bending the truth a little, because learning new dance routines can be considered studying, can't it?)

At least doing club dates around Seattle, we wouldn't have any more run-ins with people from Anacortes. So we thought!

Then the Everett Elks hired Chris and us for a special party: Anacortes Night! We debated whether to tell Patricia that we couldn't be in that program. She didn't know we were underage. That is, if she did know, she never said anything.

Maybe the dapper, good looking, clever magician could make us disappear? If only!

As we applied our makeup that dreaded night, we experimented with camouflage techniques: we slathered on the pancake base so thick there was not a trace of a freckle. Our pale, thin eyebrows grew thick and dark as we liberally applied black pencil. The bright red lip rouge seemed to reach from the tips of our noses down to our chins. for the final dramatic touch, we pulled our long hair straight back into chignons. When we were finished, we looked like we were at least forty. Even mom wouldn't have recognized us!

Betty and Bonita were already in the car when Chris stopped by to pick us up.

"Kids, ya' look like somethin' left over from Hallowe'en," our redheaded buddy remarked. "What's the big idea pretendin' to be a couple of ghouls."

"We're trying out a new look," Allene said defensively.

"The Dracula Sisters," Chris retorted.

Bonita snorted.

Lucky for us, upon our arrival at the Elks, we were hastily ushered into a back-storage closet. "Spread out and make yourselves comfortable," the jovial Elk snickered as he opened the door into the tiny room.

Chris dropped our wardrobe case in the hall and shouted at the retreating, well sudsed comedian-wanna-be, "Would you get the beer kegs and tub full of iced clams out of there."

"No can do," came the reply. "Eat, drink and …," he rounded the corner and disappeared.

"Damn joker," swore our usually mild-mannered emcee as he shoved the case into the crammed full closet.

Betty bolted after the tipsy Elk, "Buddy! Get us a clothes rack."

"This is great. Just great!" Bonita groaned.

"With any luck, everyone from Anacortes will be sloshed before the show starts," Allene whispered to me.

"Don't plan on it," I shot back. All I wanted was for the night to be over.

Our opening number was perfect. The Oriental. With its billowing chiffon sleeves and even more chiffon hanging off the hat and trailing over our shoulders, our costumes were a perfect camouflage. Especially when the filmy material flew across our faces as we twirled across the stage and when we hid behind Bonita in the Buddha sequence.

"Whew! We got through that one safely enough," my sister sighed as we rushed back to the closet dressing room.

"And we didn't trip once. Gosh, it's hard to see where you're going with …"

"What's with you two? You came that close to running into me," Bonita complained, indicating a fraction of an inch between her thumb and forefinger.

"Oops. Sorry!"

"Well, look where you're going!"

Betty managed to get the clothes rack for our costumes, but Chris had no luck getting the beer and clams out of our space. It was a tight squeeze as we tried to avoid tripping over the obstacles -- or worse, dropping a costume into one of them.

Before she joined him for some magic tricks, Bonita had a quick change to make while Chris did his monolog. Betty helped her with snaps and zippers, while Allene and I backed up close to the wall to give them room.

Jammed into that unventilated, hot, little space waiting to go on in the finale, the combined smell of the beer and the clams had made me feel dizzy and a little queasy. When I tried to get some air by sticking my head out the door, a drunk barged in.

"Sorry, fella, this ain't the Gents," Betty yelled. He sheepishly slunk away down the hall. I reluctantly closed the door.

Our final number was the football routine. In those brief outfits, we had no flowing sleeves or hats to hide our faces. Good thing there was plenty of action.

While the four of us were moving so fast and performing all the acrobatics, it wouldn't be easy for anyone to recognize us. At least, that thought carried the two of us through the number. Of course, it helped tremendously that the room was blue with cigarette smoke by then. Amid cheers and whistles, we took our bows and rushed back to the closet to change.

My one thought was, get out of there on the double.

Uh, oh! The friendly Elk who had ushered us in was waiting for us in the makeshift dressing room, "Want to come out for a nightcap?"

Betty flattened him with, "NOT ON YER LIFE, FELLA!"

Chapter 16

Getting Together with our Neighbors

Several of the acts from the Palomar stayed over to take advantage of December's active casuals (read club dates) scene.

"Three or four jobs a week and we make about as much as we would doing two or three shows every night of the week in a nightclub," Lou proclaimed. "This is sweet!"

Our veteran show business neighbors often had informal get-togethers after work; these were usually potlucks. Being the newcomers, hardly out of the amateur stage, we felt lucky to be included. There was always plenty of good-humored conversation, critiquing of other acts, descriptions of the good and bad places to work and, of course, lots of food.

This time we were gathered in Phil and Mimi's living room. It was Monday and most of us on the third floor weren't working that night. Earlier in the evening, we'd been to a second run theater on First Avenue to see a John Wayne movie in which Lou had a featured role.

"You didn't know I co-starred with the famous Western star, did you? Of course, this was a World War II story set in a submarine," he said with a shrug of his shoulders.

"It was a good part, Lou, but co-star? You're padding your billing a bit, my friend," his partner said shaking her head.

"Well, I got to use my own name. How about that scene where I describe my dad and uncle's vaudeville act?"

"I was impressed," Phil assured him from the kitchenette. He and Lou had struck up a friendship right off the bat when they met while sharing the same bill at the Palomar for a couple of weeks. One of their favorite topics of discussion was Alaska, because they discovered they'd been working in Anchorage, Alaska, at the same time just a month or so before the Palomar engagement.

"How did you miss meeting each other in Alaska; Anchorage isn't that big a place, is it?" I inquired.

"It actually is a pretty good-sized city, angel, but that wasn't the reason. Working three shows a night, seven nights a week with matinee performances out at Elmendorf Air Base on Sunday afternoons didn't leave much time for socializing. We struggled to get enough time to eat and sleep on that schedule," Lou answered.

"Amen," chimed in Mimi. "Phil and I were appearing downtown at the Aleutian Gardens, working the same grueling schedule, I might add. Only way we could have caught their show out at the Last Chance, had we had the time, you understand, would have been to take a cab. The price of cabs is out of sight up there."

"Yeah. Pity we had to leave our car in Seattle. Airlines charge extra to carry vehicles in the luggage compartment, you know," Phil added with a chuckle.

I wanted to hear more about this arctic territory that was contending with the tropical Hawaiian Islands to become our next state. "What's it like up there? Did you see any prospectors or the Northern Lights? When does the sun set?"

"Whoa! Hold on there, kiddo. Take a breath," Phil bellowed. "Lou, how about you and Camille answering her questions? I've got to concentrate on the dinner preparations."

"Well, kids, we didn't see much of the town beyond our hotel and the club, but I was bowled over by the gorgeous mountains around the place. Missed the sunsets completely."

"I'll take over, honey," Camille interjected. "If you're thinking about performing up there, let me point out, it's not a place you want to be without a male companion for protection. The patrons of the Alaskan clubs can be pretty rough. There are at least ten men for every woman; most of those men are loggers, fishermen and, yes, prospectors. Those are lonely occupations. When they come into the city they are looking for a high time with booze and women."

"That's right," agreed Mimi. "In other words, lone females beware."

Allene observed, "So, Alaska is not only expensive; it's dangerous. We sure don't want to go there, Pat."

I hadn't said I wanted to go there to work. Still, meeting gold prospectors and seeing the Northern Lights would be exciting.

Phil broke in to say, "Changing the subject a bit, Lou, were you in town when the Herods' show was knocking them dead at the vaudeville house?"

"The name isn't familiar. What kind of act do they have?"

"It's a miniature revue; damnedest thing you ever saw," Phil answered as he fished hot dogs out of a cauldron of boiling water on the stove. "Ouch!"

"What happened, honey?" Mimi inquired from the living room.

"Got splashed on. Nothing serious. Just third-degree burns."

"I have some Unquentine salve in our room. It'll only take me a minute to run over and get it," Camille offered.

"Naw. I'll put some ice on it." He came out to set the plateful of dogs on the table. "Anyway, as I was saying, only six people, mind you, and they do this fast paced musical show with comedy, dancing girls, puppets, concert violin and --"

"Hold on there a minute, buddy. Did you say concert violin? There can't be much demand for that kind of performance in our racket," Lou protested.

"Wrong!" said Phil as he took time out to slice a bun, slip in a wiener, add a splash of mustard topped off with a few pickle slices, then, with a flourish, hand it to Mimi. Turning back to Lou, he continued, "After half an hour of jokes, comedy skits, chorus and specialty routines, Jat pulls out his fiddle and launches into one of the Liszt rhapsodies without a word of introduction. It really showed off his skill. First timers to his show are bowled over; they're not expecting a classically trained musician. And get this, he finishes up his set playing Jerome Kenn's dreamy *Smoke Gets in Your Eyes*. The guy's a master!"

"That's high praise coming from a musical pro like yourself."

"Yeah, well he deserves it. Jat was a child prodigy, toured all over the States and Europe before he was a teenager."

"So, he was well trained and well-traveled. What I want to know is how he became a successful nightclub act."

"So, I'll tell you. When he became an adult in the 1930s, he was out of work. There's not much demand for a grown up child prodigy in the best of times; this was the middle of the depression!" Phil paused again long enough to put together another hot dog and offer it to Camille. "He worked in vaudeville for awhile, then became an orchestra leader for a couple of years in the speakeasies. That's when I met him. Finally, he signed on as the leading man in the old style melodramas on Bryant's Showboat."

"Stop right there, buddy! Now I know you're pulling my leg. There haven't been any showboats around in a hundred years. They're deader than vaudeville, which, although it's gasping, still has a little life left in it."

"You're right about vaudeville, but you got it wrong about showboats, my friend. They haven't been gone that long. Bryant's was one of the last; it played little towns up and down the Ohio River from the early 1900s. When it ended its run in 1943 and tied up in Cincinnati for the last time, Jat had married the leading lady, Captain Billy Bryant's daughter. The two of them began touring the nightclub circuit. She's a hell of a tap dancer and can play pretty good saxophone, too."

"Really! What's the name of their act?"

"The Manhattan Cocktail Revue."

I blurted out, "That's the act Patricia was in before she started the line at the Showbox."

"Small world," Camille remarked.

Phil wasn't finished, "Anyway, Jat developed his comedy delivery skills, hired a sister singing duo to work with Betty as a three-girl chorus line and the revue was born. Since then, they've added two more chorines and they're working fifty weeks out of the year."

Worldly-wise Californian Lou softly whistled and said, "That is some success story."

Mimi daintily nibbled at her hot dog, took a sip from her glass of beer and then asked my sister, "How are things going for you two kids?"

"Working a few club dates with the line and practicing on our own act," Allene answered.

"This is your chance to follow my advice, kids. Forget working with the Sundown Girls for peanuts. Get your own act up and running while there are still a few club dates left! New Year's is just around the corner," Lou advised.

"Do you have any comedy routines?" Phil asked.

That caught us off guard. Comedy routines? We both shook our heads. Betty Grable and Lana Turner didn't do comedy. Why should we?

"Aha!" He shook his head and began fixing another hot dog, looked around and announced, "Step right up folks, whatcha waitin' for?"

"I'm waiting for the sirloin steaks," Lou said and reached for a handful of potato chips.

"Ha!" Mimi scoffed.

"Suit yourself, buddy." As he gave my sister the finished hot dog, he counseled her, "Comedy is key to having a top-notch act.

You two are naturals. The little one has big eyes. Perfect for a comedienne! You could be her straight man, Allene."

I was pretty sure my sister did not want to be anyone's straight man. Not knowing what to say, I stood up and walked over to get myself a hot dog. I was getting hungry anyway.

Camille piped up, "Phil, not everyone is comfortable doing comedy. Besides, these kids are good little dancers."

Phil was not listening. "I can see it now. Allene, you'd come on singing all by yourself -- can you sing?"

My sister nodded. She sang all the time: vacuuming, doing dishes and whenever she heard a song she knew on the radio. Like mom, she loved to sing.

"O.K. then the little one comes out and tries to join in. You sing too, don't you?"

"Sometimes," I acknowledged. Singing duets was what we did years ago when we were little kids. Our first ever performance was in 1944 at our hometown's U. S. O. singing every song we knew from that year's Rodgers and Hammerstein Broadway hit, *Oklahoma*. I still remember being up there on the stage with my sister singing to a big room filled with soldiers, sailors and marines. There was a tall, decorated and lit up Christmas tree at the back of the room. For that special evening, mom had carefully curled our hair in long ringlets and dressed us in matching pink taffeta dresses and shiny black patent leather shoes. After the program, several servicemen convinced mom we should be given dancing lessons to round out our act. Once I got into ballet and tap classes,

I became a dancer who sings. Allene is a singer who dances. That's the big difference between us.

Mimi broke in, "Phil, I don't think --"

"Hey! I just got a better idea. Listen! Allene you come out in a long white old-fashioned flannel nightie, with the cap to match. You've seen old-time pictures of 'em. Well, you're carrying this old-style lantern and you're singing. Pat you come out with a long-handled butterfly net and you sneak up behind --"

Phil is interrupted as Mr. Downing comes into the room, "Hi, gang! I was just in the area and heard a lot of noise coming from the Cornelius. I figured it was you guys and I wanted to join the party."

"What are you doing out this late?" asked Lou.

"Us Union guys have to pretty much keep the same hours you performers do. I just caught Rosita Royce and her birds at the Rivoli. While I was out, it seemed like a good time to drop by here to see what was going on."

Whew! Talk about good timing. With any luck, Phil wouldn't bring up the comedy act again.

"Besides," Mr. Downing went on, "I spent years doing an act. I still like to shoot the breeze with performers. It's hard to break old habits, you know."

"What sort of act did you have?" Allene asked

"I was a hoofer: the old soft shoe with a straw hat and cane." He stepped into the kitchenette, which had a linoleum floor, to give us a sample of his dancing style as he whistled Vincent Youman's *Tea for Two*. Who would have guessed it?

Then it hit me! I knew who he reminded me of. He looked like a middle-aged Donald O'Conner would look.

"You've still got it, old fella!" Lou exclaimed as he slapped him on the back.

Camille asked, "Do you want to grab a hot dog and a beer? There's plenty."

"Sounds great. I'm starving."

"Phil was giving the kids an idea for their act; he thinks they should add some comedy," Mimi said as she handed him a beer.

Uh Oh! I really did not want that topic to come up again.

Fortunately, Mr. Downing came to the rescue, "I'm sorry I interrupted that. Which reminds me, kids, I've found a studio in Tacoma where you can get show photos. The rates are --"

"Tacoma? The best place to get show photos is Chicago," said Phil.

The union man replied, "It's the best place, but --"

"Or Romaine's in San Francisco," Lou added. "That's where Camille and I got ours."

"But we can't afford to go to Chicago or San Francisco just to get pictures," my sister protested.

"I'm not sure we can get to Tacoma," was my observation.

"Phil, you've got to remember, these kids are just starting out. They have to get a few jobs under their belts. To do that, they need to be able to show their photos to agents," Mr. Downing explained.

"Yeah, you're right. It's a vicious circle: you can't get work unless you have decent photos and you can't afford decent photos until you get some work."

My sister slumped down into her chair. We were booked for one more club date. That was it for the Sundown Girls. Patricia had told us it's tough to book a chorus line and a magician; five person acts are too expensive. If things didn't look up for us soon, Allene planned to apply for work as a salesclerk at one of the downtown department stores during the Christmas rush. Then, at least, we'd be able to pay the rent for the rest of the month.

"This photographer better be real reasonable," Lou put in.

Mimi added, "And be sure to take your makeup case!"

Hmmmm. How did she find out about our Kennewick trip?

Mr. Downing spoke up, "Buses go to Tacoma regularly. The fellow's studio is right downtown; you can probably get off right at his door."

"We have a lot of costumes," Allene commented.

Too many to carry onto a bus. I thought of our old neighbor Mrs. Watson back in Anacortes and wished she lived here at the Cornelius. She would drive us down to Tacoma and back and love every minute of it.

Mimi interrupted my wishful thinking, "Pick out the nicest looking outfits, hon. You know, the newest and the best fitting. You won't have enough time in the studio to be making a bunch of costume changes."

"She's right, kids. Just take one or two outfits.

Chapter 17

Planning Again

"I think we have everything you want," mom said coming into our hotel room with an armful of ruffled taffeta skirts. "You'd better check. Had quite a time finding the feather cancan hats."

"Haven't you kids had enough of show business?" Dad asked as he carried in the hats on top of a bag of groceries.

"Oh, Mac, don't start on them again. Go get the dinner out of the car, so I can heat it up."

Mom hung the costumes in the closet as dad left grumbling, "So much for my opinion."

"Thanks mom," Allene said. "It's not the end of the world just because the Showbox is closed temporarily."

I wasn't as optimistic about our future as my sister seemed to be. As far as I was concerned, our future as performers looked pretty shaky. Except for the new friends we'd made, I wasn't even sure I liked being in show business all that much.

"Your dad never can look on the bright side of things. Losing his hardware store during the Depression has made him a confirmed pessimist."

"Patricia's gotten some work to tide us over," I said as cheerfully as I could, considering I had no idea how long we'd need to be tided over.

"And with the show photos, we'll be able to get work as a sister act," Allene added. "It was great you could help us with that expense. We'll pay you back."

"No need. I'm happy to do it. I wish I could do more to help. Come January I'll probably be laid off for the month. It happens every year."

"We'll be fine," Allene stated emphatically.

Mom smiled. She couldn't see that my sister had crossed her fingers behind her back.

Chapter 18

Breaking in Our Sister Act

Our last club date was a nightmare: a stag party at the Norselander! What was Patricia thinking when she booked that? Fortunately, Chris was working with us or we might not have come out alive.

The finale of the show was a stripper, which was bad enough, but she took it ALL off. All bedlam broke loose. With the drunken mob on her heels, she ran into the dressing room yelling, "Lock the door!"

Betty coolly slammed the door shut and shot the lock. That simply stopped the panting guys momentarily. They quickly began banging on the door like they wanted to break it down. Which, of course, they did! In the nick of time our magician friend stopped trying to quiet the mob and went for his car instead. From the parking area at the back of the hall, he helped us escape through the dressing room window -- costumes and all.

Mom and dad never heard about THAT show!

And we never worked with the Sundown Girls again. Bonita went on tour with Chris, as scheduled; Betty, having had it with the uncertainties of show business, packed up and went back to Phoenix; Patricia gave up on Seattle, left her husband and went to Los Angeles to try for a movie career.

As for us, Allene worked for a couple of days at the Bon Marche' during the final days of the Christmas rush, while I stayed at the apartment cooking and cleaning.

As Phil and Lou had predicted, the Tacoma photographer wasn't good. The full length photo of us in the cancan costumes was the best of the lot. The close-ups were ghastly; we looked fat and forty. Even so, Mr. Downing found a few shots he said were okay for us to use.

Then, somehow, he talked Seattle agent Len Mantel into booking us for the first week in January at the Cave Supper Club in Vancouver, B. C. That was huge! People like Nelson Eddy and Frankie Laine worked there. In the Northwest, this was the big time.

We were terrified!

Appearing with us was a popular male singing group called the Vagabonds, and, of all people, the emcee was the fellow we'd worked with in Kennewick. Rusty Colman. It's a wonder he didn't fall over when we walked into band rehearsal, but he was really nice. Even said how pleased he was to see us again. Of course, we had made him look good before. He must have figured we could do it again.

From the beginning things did not go well. At the band rehearsal I passed out the stock musical arrangements, which were mass produced printed packets of music for a variety of instruments: piano, saxes, drum, trumpets -- even violins! I had carefully marked the sections to be played in India ink and completely blacked over the sections to be skipped. The musicians, all twelve of them, took one look at my handiwork, shook their heads, rolled their eyes and laughed. Those arrangements signaled right off that we were new, green performers. If we'd been a seasoned act, like most of the Cave's entertainers, our music would have been expensive hand-written special arrangements.

The band did their best with our music, but we died every night. In spite of all our rehearsing and the coaching Lou and Camille gave us, our act was not ready for one of the biggest clubs in the territory. Smart performers do NOT break in their new acts at the best spots.

As we sat in the dressing room the night before closing I asked my sister, "Don't you wonder why the Cave's manager Isy Walters is allowing us to finish out the week. We sure aren't bringing in any crowds."

"Yes, I have thought about that. I guess he's a good friend of Phil Downing and he owes him a really big favor!"

"You're probably right."

As if dying every night were not punishment enough, the *Vancouver Sun* gave our act a dreadful review that would be read by every agent in the area. Fat chance we'd have to get another booking after that drubbing.

Sunday morning, we packed up and went home to stay. It was a pretty awful feeling knowing that before we were even out of our teens, we were washed up in show business.

I hoped I could join my class for the last semester of school.

Allene had nothing to hope for.

Chapter 19

A New Opportunity

At home, Allene took a temporary job at the dentist's office. Dr. Nicholson needed someone for a few days while his receptionist visited her family in Minnesota.

Mom, as expected, had been laid off shortly after Christmas and probably wouldn't be called back before February. She didn't let us reimburse her for the cost of our less-than-professional show pictures, so the pay we'd received for our week at the Cave was deposited into our bank account. Perhaps it would be the beginning of my sister's college fund.

I was reading Shakespeare's play, *Julius Caesar*. My friend Sharon had loaned me her English book, so I could catch up on that holiday reading assignment given by Miss Farnum. If I was prepared, perhaps I'd be allowed to rejoin my class.

"Pat," Mom called from the kitchen. "Mr. Downing is on the phone."

What could he want? Probably it was time to pay our union dues. Should we bother?

"Hello," I said none too cheerily.

"I've got great news for you kids. Jat Herod needs two dancers for his revue. One gal is taking out another line of girls for the show and the other is going out on her own as a single."

I sat down hard on the kitchen chair closest to me. Jat Herod! The Manhattan Cocktail Revue! The Halliday Sisters??

"Hello. Are you still there?"

"Y-e-e-s. I'm just not sure I heard you right."

"Listen. There is a catch to this deal. You've got to be twins. Jat thinks it's better box office than sisters."

"But we're not. Allene is almost three --"

"Doesn't matter. You two look a lot alike. You could pull it off."

Could we?

"Of course, you'll have to get a few matching outfits. There are some great sales at Fredericks and the Bon this month."

My head was spinning. I wished Allene were taking this call.

Mr. Downing was still talking. "Jat wants you to meet with his talent scout Margaret Tapping tomorrow. She's a dance instructor in the University District. After she's put you through your paces, she'll get back to him. What time should I tell her you'll be there?"

I tried to remember the train schedule. Or the bus schedule -- that would be cheaper. Or --

What was I thinking? I was going back to school!

"This is the opportunity of a lifetime for you kids. I know you will fit into his show beautifully."

You had to love this fellow's unfailing confidence in us! At least, thanks to Patricia, we already knew two of the revue's dance routines: the football and the oriental.

"Would 2:00 be O. K.?" I asked nervously, not at all sure my sister could get off work.

"Try to be at my office by 1:00."

I hung up and sat staring out the window in a daze. Things were happening so fast!

Mom was peeling potatoes at the sink, "What did Mr. Downing want?"

"Do you suppose Mrs. Watson would drive Allene and me to Seattle tomorrow?"

Chapter 20

Eureka!

"I'm so glad you needed this ride," Mrs. Watson enthused. "I've been wanting to go to the White Sales in Seattle; you've given me the excuse I needed to make the trip. Where is your appointment?"

"Downtown Seattle. You can let us off at Frederick's. It's just a few blocks from there to the AGVA office on Third Avenue," Allene told her.

My sister managed to get the day off work. Her friend Sally, home from college, had another week's vacation so she offered to fill in for her. Dr. Nicholson hadn't even made a fuss about having a replacement for his replacement.

We wore our lucky matching slack outfits over our leotards -- just like when we auditioned for Patricia at the Showbox. We weren't really superstitious, but it did give us a bit more confidence. Besides, this was all we had that was twin-like. Instead of our usual offstage ponytails, we had put our long hair into chignons to make us look sophisticated (and older as well). We'd done everything we could think of to become twins on such short notice. Still, I was scared stiff. I could tell Allene was, too. Although we didn't say anything, we knew our future was riding on this audition.

"Hi, Halliday Twins," Mr. Downing called out as we came through his office door.

"Do you really think we look enough alike?" Allene asked. Since the Cave debacle, her usual self-assurance had been at a very low ebb.

"Jat didn't specify that the twins had to be identical. You two have nothing to worry about."

Mr. Downing was quite the optimist!

On the way to Miss Tapping's studio, he told us how this audition came about. "Jat called all his major booking areas across the country: Chicago, Atlanta, Phoenix and, of course, Seattle. He told his agents in each city what he was looking for. Joe Daniels, his representative here, called me yesterday morning with the news. I got right on the phone to you."

Mr. Downing was quite a good friend, too!

He added with emphasis, "That's why I insisted that you get down here today. I don't know how much competition you have, but I do know there'll be plenty of interest. This revue is a dancer's dream!"

Suddenly, he jammed on the foot brakes as the car ahead of us slowed down to make a right turn without signaling. If we both hadn't grabbed hold of the leather hand straps hanging next to the car windows, the near collision would have knocked us off the backseat. Mr. Downing looked over his shoulder at us and asked, "You kids okay?"

We both nodded and Allene answered, "Just a little shaken up."

"Sorry. You didn't need that added excitement today. It was a close call."

Changing the subject, he continued, "Incidentally, Lou and his wife dropped by the office yesterday afternoon to pay their dues. They're on their way to Billings, Montana, for a couple of weeks at the Skyline Club. Lou asked whether I'd heard from you two, so I told him about this opportunity. He and Camille both said to wish you all the best. If you'd like to write them, they can be reached care of General Delivery in Billings."

"We sure will!" I said.

"Are Phil and Mimi still in town?" Allene inquired.

"No. Lucky stiffs! They are basking in the sun over in Honolulu. Got themselves booked into Leroy's Club out on Ala Moana for four weeks with options."

Allene murmured, "How nice."

"Sounds a lot better than Alaska," I commented remembering the conversation at our last get together with them.

Mr. Downing laughed and pulled into the parking area of a small business section near the University of Washington. "Well, this is it. Good luck! I'll be waiting for you right here. This break gives me a chance to catch up on the local news." He picked up the newspaper lying beside him on the front seat, unfolded it and settled back to read.

In the studio's reception area, a petite, dark haired woman in a black leotard greeted us. "You must be the twins Phil Downing called about. I'm Margaret Tapping. Thank you for being so prompt. We haven't much time; my classes begin in an hour."

We followed her into the studio. The dance floor, with its huge mirror lining the wall behind the barre, was almost as big as the Showbox's. Lots of room to work in. I felt better already.

For a full half hour or more she worked us: ballet, tap, acrobatics -- you name it. The whole time I did my best to keep in mind Patricia's instructions that dancing should look carefree and easy.

Finally, Miss Tapping said, "That will do. I'll call Jat when I get a break later today. He's vacationing in Florida this week, but he's staying close to the telephone. I hope this will work out for you. It's a wonderful show."

Hmmm. Did she say that to everyone who tried out with her? Besides being a worry wart, I seemed to be working on being a skeptic, too.

"How did it go?" Mr. Downing asked as we got back into his car.

Allene answered, "We don't know yet. She only told us that she'll be calling Mr. Herod today."

"I'll phone him first thing in the morning and get the results. You'll hear from me -- one way or the other -- as soon as I know his decision." He started up the car and pulled out of the parking lot.

"Where would you like to be dropped off?"

Not knowing whether we had the jobs or not, it wasn't easy for me to get excited about spending time and money shopping for identical outfits we may never need. But my sister sounded like her old self again as she quickly answered, "Frederick's. We're meeting our neighbor there, so we can shop for the new clothes we'll need."

Was she really that confident we'd be hired?

As he dropped us off at the store, he reiterated, "I'll call you as soon as I hear from Jat."

Mrs. Watson's arms were already full of packages when we found her in the linen department as planned. "How did your audition go?"

"We don't know whether we're hired or not, but we did our best," I said.

Allene came back with, "How many twins could there be auditioning, Pat? Think positive!"

So, the three of us spent the rest of the afternoon shopping. As Allene put it, "We might as well. We have to be prepared for our big break." She had been a pretty good Girl Scout in her younger days.

First thing in the morning, Mr. Downing -- always as good as his word -- gave us the verdict.

In less than a week, we were kissing our parents goodbye at the Mount Vernon train depot and beginning the cross country train trip to Biloxi, Mississippi. That was where we would join Jat Herod and the other members of the Manhattan Cocktail Revue to start rehearsals on Monday. The Halliday Twins had one week to learn four of the revue's chorus numbers before opening at the Stables Supper Club on the beach there.

Maybe two of the routines will be a snap to us, thanks to Patricia!

Acknowledgements

Sincere thanks to Dixie Rogerson for the delightful artwork on the cover.

I am grateful for the assistance and encouragement I received from Sharon Ripp, Jody Chadderton, Eva Turner, Mark Clendon, Phyllis Luvera Ennes, and my editors Annabelle Barrette and Rachel Johnson at Village Books.

Circa 1995. Reprinted with the kind permission of the Journal of the San Juan Islands

Afterword

Joining the Manhattan Cocktail Revue in 1953 led us to years of performing in nightclubs and television all over the United States. Those years were fun and filled with adventures, which have been recorded in the upcoming book, *Diary of a Dancin' Girl.*

www.ingramcontent.com/pod-product-compliance
Lightning Source LLC
Chambersburg PA
CBHW051405290426
44108CB00015B/2167